I-SEARCH, YOU SEARCH,
WE ALL LEARN TO RESEARCH

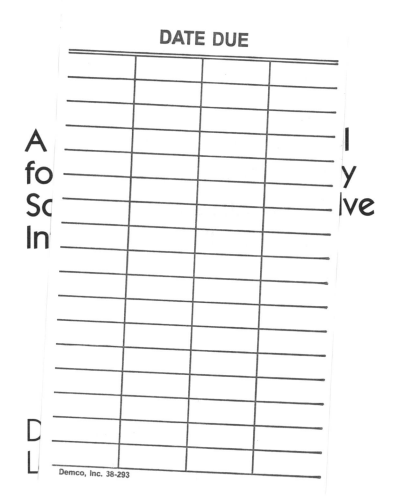

DATE DUE

Demco, Inc. 38-293

HOW-TO-DO-IT MANUALS
FOR LIBRARIANS

NUMBER 97

NEAL-SCHUMAN PUBLISHERS, INC.
New York, London

Published by Neal-Schuman Publishers, Inc.
100 Varick Street
New York, NY 10013

The paper used in this publication meets the minimum requirements of American National Standard for Information Sciences—Permanence of Paper for Printed Library Materials, ANSI Z39.48–1992.

Printed and bound in the United States of America.

ISBN 1–55570–381–X

Library of Congress Cataloging-in-Publication Data

Duncan, Donna.
    I-Search, you search, we all to learn to research : a how-to-do-it manual for teaching elementary school students to solve information problems / Donna Duncan, Laura Lockhart.
        p.   cm. — (How-to-do-it manuals for librarians ; no. 97)
    ISBN 1-5557-381-X (alk. paper)
      1. Library orientation for school children—United States.   2. Report writing.   I. Lockhart, Laura. II. Title. III. How-to-do-it manuals for libraries ; no. 97.

Z711.2.D86 2000
372.13'028'1—dc 21   99-089993

DEDICATION

*To Bob for his unfailing and unconditional love; to Laura
for giving me the treasured gift of being her mentor; to Lisa
who opens doors of beauty for others; to Mallory for
strengthening my desire to make learning exciting for
children; to Jordan and Greg for being a part of our family;
and to my mom and dad for their loving support.*

DONNA DUNCAN

*To Jordan for his patience, encouragement, and love; to
Mallory for the joy, hope, and love she has brought to our
family; to Mom and Dad for their immense support and
confidence in me; and to Lisa and Greg for their loving
contributions to our family.*

LAURA LOCKHART

CONTENTS

LIST OF FIGURES

ACKNOWLEDGMENTS

First and foremost, we would like to thank our husbands, Bob and Jordan, for their loving support and patience of this project from inception to completion.

We also want to thank Mallory Margaret. The contract for the book was signed in July, and we found out in September that Mallory would arrive the following May. So, she has been present during the whole writing process. Her birth has dictated the writing schedule around feeding and play time. Her presence is a wonderful reminder that it is important to write a book that will help children develop life skills that will contribute to their social well being and the democratic way of life.

Dr. Barbara Stein, our editor, has energized us with her commitment to this project. We would not have taken the leap to actually write about our experiences with the I-Search research model without her support and encouragement

We are indebted to the many publishers and authors who gave us permission to use portions of their work. We discovered a new community of lifelong and supportive learners as we worked with these people.

We appreciate our many teaching colleagues, administrators, parents and students, and the Mesquite ISD Library Services staff who have shared our journey and have been excited about the discoveries that result from I-Searching.

PREFACE

What is an I-Search? It originates from the word *research*, which makes most of us think of schools, universities, and labs. While these settings lend themselves to research, I-Search is not a word or process only for the educational setting. Everyone I-Searches in many different ways and for many different reasons. Ken Macrorie, author of *The I-Search Paper*, describes the I-Search as a project where a person conducts a search to find out something he needs to know for his own life and writes the story of his adventure (1988). It is an inquiry-based process that compels students to move away from the traditional research report format in which they restate old information (Macrorie, 1988). We found that this process empowers our students and brings out their curiosity and love of learning while laying a foundation for building a community of lifelong learners.

We I-Search when we shop for a new car, decide on a college major, look for a new job, and try to find the right area in which to live. We all have questions we want answered and some of us want and need the opportunity to find answers to questions we do not even know we have. I-Searching is fun, rewarding, and essential. What better gift to give our children than the ability to research a problem, whether it be the best bike to buy or writing a history term paper? Giving our children the lifelong ability to solve information problems and make well-thought-out decisions is priceless.

How does an I-Search accomplish these goals? The past several years we have researched, questioned, and concluded that children learn best when they are given opportunities for exploration and to make decisions about their learning. This type of learning is based on Bloom's Taxonomy of higher-order thinking. Using the I-Search process, children move from a basic knowledge level of learning to the higher levels of analyzing, synthesizing, and evaluation when working with information problems. With this approach, students discover the ability to:

- Develop their own questions.
- Seek answers through research and interviews.
- Record in note form the information that they find.
- Produce and present products based on their research.
- Evaluate those products and processes through the use of rubrics and other evaluation instruments.

This utilization of Bloom's Taxonomy has provided a solid theoretical base to construct an information problem-solving model to guide the I-Search process. *I-Search, You Search, We All Learn to Research* is geared specifically to elementary students. This book will help a variety of educators understand and develop discovery opportunities for their students:

- Undergraduate and graduate students enrolled in elementary education and library/information studies programs.
- Elementary administrators, team leaders, curriculum directors, and subject coordinators.
- Practicing elementary teachers and librarians.

This book is organized in five sections. Each section represents one of the five steps of the information problem-solving model children employ with the I-Search process. This five-step process will also help educators organize the I-Search unit. These steps are:

Step 1: What do I want to know?
Step 2: Where can I find the answers?
Step 3: How will I record the information that I find?
Step 4: How will I show what I learned?
Step 5: How will I know I did a good job?

This book shows "how to" teach the I-Search process from start to finish. It is organized in such a way that will help students and teachers who are new to information problem solving and the I-Search. It will also be helpful to those who would like to implement the philosophy a little at a time and find strategies that will be of use in current units of study. Finally, for those who have done I-Searches with their elementary students, we will provide some additional ideas and suggestions that may be helpful.

This educational journey facilitates meaningful experiences and empowers all those involved. We believe that this adventure in learning will lay a solid foundation and equip children with the confidence and competence to become lifelong learners and effective users of information.

SECTION I:

WHAT DO I WANT TO KNOW

1 CHOOSING THE TOPIC

In this chapter...

- Lesson: Introducing the I-Search Project
- The Learning Log
- Skimming and Scanning
- Library Skills
- Lesson: Why I Chose This Topic

"Giving students choices is as much a fundamental principle of good teaching as it is a specific intrapersonal teaching strategy" (Armstrong, 1994: 83). Choice drives the I-Search unit. Students choose their topic, their best resources, and how they will show what they learned. "Making these choices is like lifting weights. The more frequently students can choose from a group of options the thicker their 'responsibility muscles' become" (Armstrong, 1994: 83). The following are strategies, ideas, and techniques that will yield stronger and more responsible students.

Choosing a topic may seem like a very simple thing to do, and it is for some. However, the topic needs to be one that is well-thought-out and is of great interest to the student. As we have researched and studied the needs of our students each year, we discovered that the topic decision has a critical role in determining the success of the research. As a result, each year we have dedicated more and more time to facilitating the topic choice with the students.

We have included suggested lessons in each chapter that will help teach the I-Search unit. Embedded in these lessons are student examples, stories, and notes that help to show how we strive to create a community of learners. We have attempted to include what we know about good teaching in these lessons. The lessons are flexible, however, and should be adjusted, modified, and/or extended to meet the levels and needs of the students.

LESSON: INTRODUCING THE I-SEARCH PROJECT

MATERIALS NEEDED AND ADVANCE PREPARATION
- Copy of newspaper article "Ring of Truth"
- Joanna Cole's book *On the Bus With Joanna Cole: A Creative Autobiography*
- Transparency of Research Planner
- Transparency of Interest Map.
- Copy of Interest Map for each student.
- Overhead pens in at least three different colors
- Overhead projector
- Transparency of Possible I-Search Topics Sheet
- Copy of Possible I-Search Topics Sheet for each student

OBJECTIVE
Students will be introduced to the I-Search and begin thinking of possible topics of study.

ANTICIPATORY SET AND INTRODUCTION
- There are several activities that help students begin thinking about topics they may want to research. Read the newspaper article published by the *Dallas Morning News* in 1995 called "The Ring of Truth" by Douglas Holt (Figure 1.1) to make a real-world connection to the I-Search. This article is about a third grader, named Avril, who finds a Rose Bowl ring while watching a Dallas Cowboys' football game at Texas Stadium. With the help of her teacher and librarian she conducts research to find the owner. The story concludes with Avril returning the ring to Washington Redskins' safety Keith Taylor. He was so appreciative he gave her tickets to the next Cowboys-Redskins game. The article serves as a wonderful real-world example of the importance of research and information problem solving. It's also a great lesson in the life skills of perseverance, initiative, and integrity. Discuss all of these issues and then post it on the wall as a real-world reminder of what I-Searching is and its importance.

Note: A bulletin board or other empty space can be used to post the learning that will be done throughout the I-Search.

Figure 1.1 — Ring of Truth

When honest 8-year-old returns a keepsake, she gets to meet a hero and to be one as well. By Douglas Holt: Staff Writer of the *Dallas Morning News*

Eight-year-old Avril Terry spotted a small gleam of gold while walking down a Texas Stadium ramp after the San Francisco 49ers trounced the Cowboys a few weekends ago.

She thought it was a candy wrapper.

It was something quite different: a treasured 1984 Rose Bowl championship ring belonging to Washington Redskins safety Keith Taylor, who made eight solo tackles in a 27-23 victory over Dallas Oct. 1.

How the weighty gold, sapphire, and diamond ring got there is a story in itself. But how Avril, a third grader at the Episcopal School of Dallas, located the ring's rightful owner is a lesson in honesty, in perseverance, and even in being a super sleuth at the library.

Ten days of research and a half dozen long distance telephone calls later, Mr. Taylor, 30, called Avril to thank her. He invited the girl, her parents, and a friend to attend the Cowboys-Redskins rematch on Sunday.

The night before the game, Avril is scheduled to meet Mr. Taylor in person. She'll hand over the ring, and he'll hand over four tickets. Mr. Taylor said he's thinking about bringing his young friend an early Christmas present, too.

The episode has made her a celebrity among her third-grade pals.

"Everybody was like jumping on me, like, 'Get me an autograph!'," she said, still in a school uniform at her parents North Dallas home.

"It was pretty neat because everybody was saying, 'Oh my gosh, you're sooo lucky. You're sooo lucky.'"

It was luck that Avril found the ring. But Keith Taylor knows that it took more than luck for him to get it back.

"Somebody else might have picked it up and said, 'Oh, I'll keep it,' or 'I'll take it to a pawnshop,'" Mr. Taylor said Wednesday by telephone from his home in Sterling, Va. "With all the problems we have in the world and with kids today, to meet somebody that nice and that honest is just unbelievable. It just reflects on how her parents are raising her."

Mr. Taylor, it turns out, wasn't the one who lost the ring. After returning from the Rose Bowl in 1984, where he played as a University of Illinois freshman, he gave the token to his father for safekeeping.

John Taylor of Pennsauken, NJ, has two sons who play professional football: Keith and his older brother, John, the 49ers' wide receiver best known for nailing a 10-yard touchdown pass from Joe Montana to beat Cincinnati in the 1989 Super Bowl.

The father came to Dallas to watch John play Nov. 12. He wore Keith's Rose Bowl ring and prayed when he came home without it that the ring was merely lost in his baggage or stuck in a pocket somewhere. He hadn't told his son it was lost.

The day after the game, Avril's mother, Helen Terry, called Texas Stadium to report that her daughter had found the ring. But the real action started when Avril took the ring to school.

Avril's teacher, Linda McSwain, sent Avril to the library to find who owned the keepsake.

The ring came with many clues. It says: "BIG TEN CHAMPIONS — ROSE BOWL 1984." It has an orange Fighting Illini helmet on the side. It even shows a last name, "Taylor."

Librarian Bonnie Tolleffson and her assistant, Mary Margaret Underklofler, suggested books to look up and places to call. But they let Avril do most of the talking.

Avril called the University of Illinois Alumni Association. The group's last contact for Mr. Taylor was with the New Orleans Saints. When she found that he had left the Saints, the librarians called several NFL associations. They got the number for Mr. Taylor's agent and let Avril call it.

She is a ruddy-faced girl who prefers Reebok basketball shoes to the saddle shoes of her uniform, who says she loves "to play football with the boys at recess."

A clear speaker, Avril enunciates each word she says. You can easily imagine her calmly explaining her situation to professional football player agent Walter Norton in Boston.

"I said my name, where I'm from, what grade I'm in, how old I am, and where I live," she said. "I said: 'I found his ring…'"

The ring memorializes a stinging defeat for the Illini who lost 45-9 to UCLA that year. Still, Keith Taylor calls it "part of my history."

And he gets to keep it because one kid in Dallas decided to ignore the not-so-golden rule of the playground finders, keepers, losers, weepers. Her reasoning is disarmingly simple.

"It was a Rose Bowl ring, and it had to be something really important to somebody," she said. "They would really want it back."

Reprinted with permission of the Dallas Morning News

CONNECTION AND INPUT

- Review the "Research Planner" information problem-solving organizer (see Figure 1.2).

Note: We use this information planner in many ways throughout the year. For example, when teaching a unit on Indians we use the planner to organize the research we do as a class. If students are not familiar with an information planner, then the I-Search is a good way to introduce them to the process.

We have found that one way to review the Research Planner is to discuss how Avril used the information problem-solving model to find the answers to her questions. We ask the students to brainstorm and discuss each of the steps and how they apply to Avril's research.

- What do I want to know? Find the owner of the Rose Bowl ring.
- Where can I find the answers? People: teacher, librarians, parents, football agents. Sources: clues from the ring, books, phone book, University of Illinois, New Orleans Saints, NFL Association.
- How will I record the information that I find? The newspaper does not go into detail about this, but have the students brainstorm possible ways she could have recorded her information. This discussion could be based on what you have been using to record information in the classroom. In our case, we used Note Sheets.
- How will I show what I learned? By returning the ring to its rightful owner.
- How will I know that I did a good job? Question number one was answered. The reaction of the owner of the ring also determined how well the job was done (the owner was very appreciative).

This activity will reiterate the connection and importance of using information problem-solving tools to find the answers to real-world problems.

CONTINUED CONNECTION AND INTRODUCTION

Another wonderful source used to introduce students to information problem solving is the book called *On the Bus With Joanna Cole; A Creative Autobiography*. Many students have heard of the *Magic School Bus* series and are able to make an immediate connection to the author. In her autobiography, Joanna writes of her experiences in

Figure 1.2

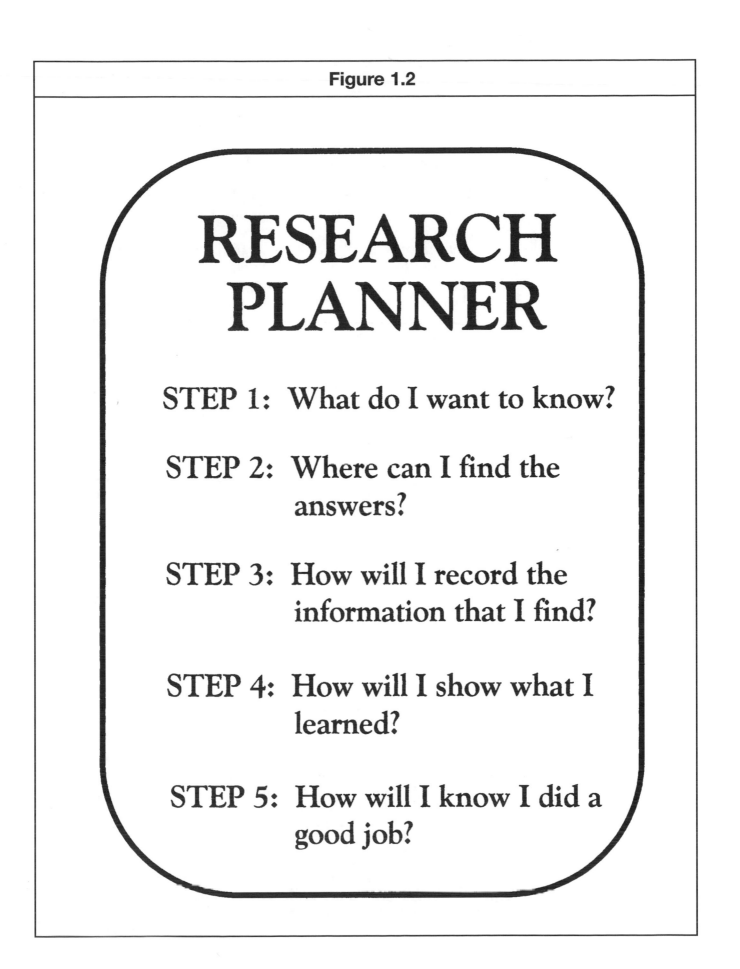

writing science books. She describes her process in marvelous detail and with enthusiasm. Joanna serves as our model of a reader, writer, and researcher who loves her work and communicates it beautifully. Her words are an inspiration throughout the I-Search journey.

- Introduce Joanna's book and read the first excerpt on how she chooses topics to research. Chapter Two of her book is appropriately titled "Getting a Good Idea." She shares examples of how she gets ideas for writing nonfiction books. These include subjects about which she has always been curious, editors' suggestions, ideas from books she has written before, and personal experiences.
- Discuss how and why she chooses topics.
- Round out this introductory work by sharing past I-Search papers. As these papers are read, discuss the reasons each person chose their topic (see Figures 1.3 and 1.4).

Kevin, a fifth grader, wrote his paper on "The Inside and Outside of a Diesel Truck." He had become fascinated by diesel trucks because his neighbor had one and he wanted to know more about them. Jessica, a third grader, had a pet cat and just recently got a kitten. She wanted to know more about how to take care of them so she wouldn't "lose" them.

By now, students are popping with ideas for their I-Search projects. Ask them to be patient and work through a few activities that will help them learn more about themselves and possibly even other topics.

MODELING THE INTEREST MAP

Modeling for students has increasingly become an important part of our teaching. We have learned that whatever we are asking our students to do we should be willing to do ourselves. In the reading and writing workshops, we constantly strive to model our own reading, responses, and writing in progress. We have found that sharing and encouraging our students to share, not only teaches them the process, but also creates a personalized, positive, and safe community of learners. As a result, the "Interest Map" (Figure 1.5) is the first activity that we do together. First, the process is modeled on the overhead in a think-aloud fashion. For example, we talk through each step so that the students will be able to see what and how we are thinking so they can physically see possible ways to come up with ideas for themselves. The Interest Map helps the students dig a little deeper into their own experiences and interests to find possible I-Search topics. The follow-

Figure 1.3

Kevin Jones
LA S-2
February 27, 1995

THE INSIDE AND OUTSIDE OF A DIESEL TRUCK

What I Knew Before I Started My I-Search

Before I started my I-Search, I knew that trucks that go long distance have a bed in them. All trucks have CB's in them. They also have radios. And they run on diesel fuel. Trucks have orange lights on top of the trucks to tell other drivers how wide the truck is.

Why I am Writing the Paper

The reason is because I had never looked at the inside of a diesel truck. Some people were moving in across the street from us and the man had a diesel truck. So my dad took me over and I got to look inside the truck. The man's name was Mr. Lacey. He said that he would take me for a ride. And after that I just fell in love with the trucks. Now I go over there when I want and he teaches me about diesel trucks. He even let me drive it, with him sitting next to me of course.

The Search

On my search, I went to our school library. Mrs. Lockhart helped me. We found one book about diesels, but it did not give me any information. So I found another book but I still got no information. So I thought I was not getting anywhere on my I-Search. The next time I went back to the library, there were only two books left about diesels, so I got them. They had the information I was looking for, but not enough. I then decided that I needed to do an interview. So I interviewed my neighbor across the street because he drives diesel trucks. I received a lot of information from Mr. Lacey.

Then I needed to put my information in order. I then bought some film and I started taking pictures of diesel trucks. I took pictures of the inside, pictures of the outside, pictures of the trailer, pictures of the motor, and I took pictures of the CB. This helped me compare the different types of trucks.

Next I went to a truck dealership. I got to look at a brand new diesel truck. They had electrical fences around them for safe keeping. I also went to a truck stop to take pictures of different types of trucks.

What I Learned

I learned that a brand new diesel all clean will cost around or more than $50,000.00. There are

Figure 1.3 *(continued)*

Figure 1.3 — *Continued*

also two types of trucks. A cabover and a conventional truck. A cabover is a truck with the cab sitting over the engine. Also called a "flatface." A conventional truck is where the engine is placed in front of the driver's compartment.

Diesel truck engines are very powerful and cost a lot of money. The range of the horse power of the motor is around 300 to 500 horsepower.

A driver that goes long distance and across country has a bed in their truck. Truck drivers that have a sleeping compartment call their trucks a "Pajama Wagon."

A truck also has what is called a fifth wheel. And it has to be greased all over so the trailer will hook up smoothly. The trailer is put on top of the fifth wheel and latched down. There are also three types of trailers. A tank trailer, a flatbed, and an enclosed trailer. All for carrying heavy loads. Trucks also have 18 wheels. This is why they are called eighteen wheelers. The truck and the trailer combined make 18 wheels.

There are many types of diesel trucks. There is the International, the Peterbilt, the Kenworth, the Freightliner, the Mac, and many more.

Truck drivers are also called truckers. Truckers also talk on their CB radios. When a trucker sees police he tells other drivers. They call the police "Smokeys" or "Bandits." The truck has a special button that needs to be pushed before the engine will start. The driver needs a special license to drive a diesel truck.

It takes a special skill to drive a diesel truck. Most trucks have 10 or more gears to shift. Mr. Lacey's truck has 15 gears. He said his worst fear when driving his truck is to turn it over. That can easily happen if he does not get enough sleep for he does long hauls. There are many rules that he has to follow in order to avoid accidents.

Diesel trucks also have their own truck wash. A truck driver takes pride in his truck when he keeps it clean. It is like home to some drivers for they go on long trips like Mr. Lacey. He washes and polishes his truck regularly. It takes him the whole day to clean and polish his truck. I got to help him polish the chrome on his truck. It was hard work.

The inside and outside of a diesel truck is made up of two main parts. The truck itself and the trailer. But by having all the other parts such as a bed, CB, a strong motor, and a good wash is what makes a good looking truck.

Bibliography

Mr. Lacey. Personal Interview.
	13 February, 1995
Mark, Rich. *Diesel Trucks.*
	United States: Enterprises, 1978
Ruth, Robert. *Trucks and Trucking.*
	United States: 1982
Wolfe, Robert. *The Truck Book.*
	Minneapolis: Carolrhoda Books, Inc., 1981

Figure 1.4

My I-Search on Cats

Written and Illustrated by Jessica Christensen

Dedicated to my mom because she helped me so much.

#1 MOM

1.   Why I Chose This Topic

I chose cats because I have two at home. I got my first cat when I was one year old. I also want to know how to take better care of my cats. I will get a new one. But if I can take better care of them I will not lose them.

2.   What I Knew

I know a cat should not leave it's mom until it is 8 weeks old. When you buy a cat under 8 weeks old you're taking a big responsibility. Some times cats have to stay longer than 8 weeks. But when you get a cat under 8 weeks you have to teach it to use the litter box. There are other things you have to teach them too.

3.   The Search

When I started the search I didn't find much. But my mom took me to the Temple Public Library. The book that I got didn't give me any information.

On April 16th I found two books. They were called *Kitties* and the encyclopedia. They answered some of my questions. I felt happy.

On April 18th my mom took me to my cat's veterinarian Dr. Bill Glass. He was able to answer all of my questions.

4.   What I Learned

I learned many things about cats during my I-Search. I was able to answer all of my questions.

I learned cats drink by turning their tongues under forming a cup to lap their food or water.

Cats can live up to 18 to 19 years. But if a cat isn't well taken care of it will live up to 12 or 13 years.

Cats can run up to 30 miles per hour. I think that's great.

Cats are very intelligent. Most can be trained to do many things. When a cat is happy it will purr,

5.

play, or hold it's tail high. When it's sad it will look outside. When it's mad it will want to be left alone.

I liked researching about my topic. I'll be able to use what I learned when I become a cat veterinarian.

6.   Project and Presentation

I made a poster to show what I learned about cats. To make my poster I bought yellow and blue posters. The blue was for practice. My mom and I did not like it so my mom helped me with the blue one. I took pictures of my cat to show what I learned. We took the blue poster and cut it for around the pictures I had taken.

On April 25th 1997 I presented my project. When Mrs. Lockhart called my name I was scared at first. But I did fine after I started.

7.   Self Evaluation

During my I-Search I learned how to use the card catalog. I will be able to use what I learned again when I am older. I feel like I did good on my project. I included all the things I found out about cats. The thing I did best was eye contact. Next time I could do my volume better. The thing I liked most about doing this project was making my poster.

8.   Bibliography
1. Glass, Bill, Interview, April 16th, 1997
2. McGinnis, Terri, "Cats", *The World Book Encyclopedia,* 1990.
3. Vrbava, Zuza, *Kittens,* 1990.

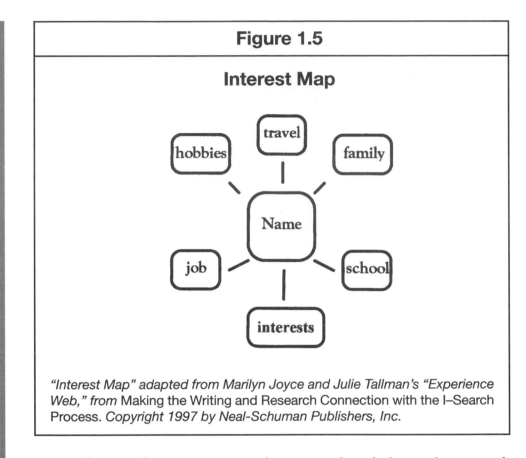

Figure 1.5

Interest Map

"Interest Map" adapted from Marilyn Joyce and Julie Tallman's "Experience Web," from Making the Writing and Research Connection with the I–Search Process. *Copyright 1997 by Neal-Schuman Publishers, Inc.*

ing is the step-by-step process that is used to help students work through the activity.

- Discuss with students that the Interest Map to help clarify the choices they have made while also helping those who do not yet have topics. Pass out an Interest Map to each student.
- Model for students by making balloons around each milestone, listing the first two or three things that pop into your head. These could include people, places, or incidents related to each milestone. Have students repeat the process with their own Interest Map.
- Create a second layer for each balloon consisting of experiences and questions concerning the milestones. Students repeat the process.
- Model studying the Web and choosing the top three topics about which you would like to know more. Put a star by the top three. Students repeat the process.
- Rank the choices from number one to number three. List them at the bottom of the page. Students repeat the process. See Figure 1.6 for an example of a completed Interest Map.

Figure 1.6

Interest Map

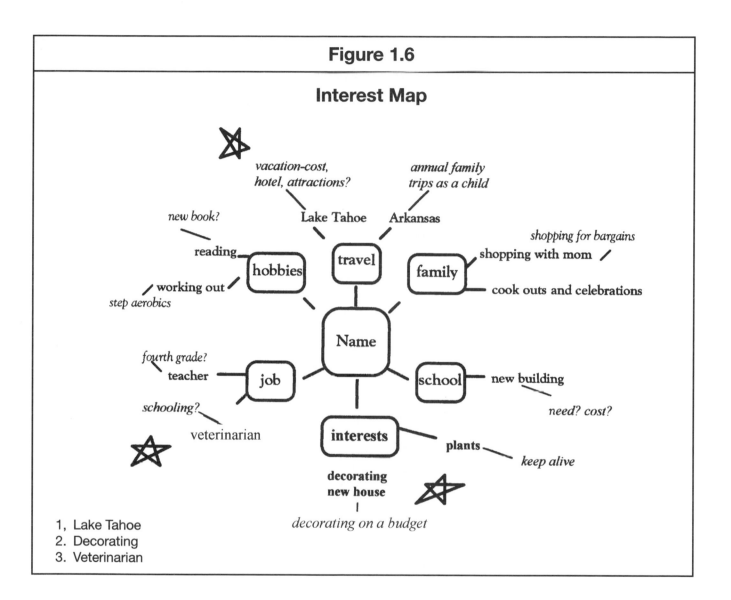

1. Lake Tahoe
2. Decorating
3. Veterinarian

At this point, the students have done a lot of thinking about their experiences and interests, so it's time to talk. Talking about what has been done so far serves two purposes. First, it helps to verbalize the thoughts and, second, it will be preliminary work for the writing activity that will follow.

GUIDED PRACTICE AND GROUP WORK

- The teacher shares the top three topics and the reason she has chosen these particular subjects. Give personal reasons.
- Ask students to think about each of their topics one at a time. Have them think about the personal reasons they would like to know more about these topics.

- Have the students turn to their partner and discuss their top three possible topics. Encourage them to give personal reasons for choosing each one.

MODELING AND INDEPENDENT PRACTICE

Students have internalized and verbalized their thoughts and now are ready to write. The "Possible I-Search Topics" sheet is used to help students uncover their interests and begin to narrow their possibilities (see Figure 1.7).

- Model writing on each possible topic. Read and think aloud thoughts.
- Have students write on their three topics.

CLOSURE

- Have students re-read their work and make corrections.
- Tell students that this preliminary work is the beginning of a wonderful adventure in learning and growing. Let them know that they will have additional time to think about their topics. Encourage them to think about their topics during the day and at home. Reiterate that it is important to choose a topic that is of great interest to them.

The above lesson may cover several days. This is OK because students need to spend time thinking and internalizing who they are and what they want to know. They will be spending a great deal of time and energy with their topic. Consequently, it is important that the topic is very meaningful to them.

Figure 1.7

Possible I-Search Topics

Name_____

- My first choice of a topic is   because

- My second choice of a topic is   because

- My third choice of a topic is   because

THE LEARNING LOG

Robin Fogarty, in her book *The Mindful School: How to Teach for Metacognitive Reflection*, describes "Learning Logs" as written entries that relate to the learning at hand. She states that Learning Logs could be separate booklets used specifically and solely for logging student thinking. They also may be a separate section of another notebook that is designated for log entries. She explains that the key to Learning Logs is that the student's writing is directly tied to the learning of the moment (1994: 14). She cites Peter Elbow as the pioneer in the use of Learning Logs as a metacognitive tool for students. He finds that the log is a viable tool for students as they accept more and more responsibility for their own learning (Elbow cited in Fogarty, 1994:15).

Over the years, we have adapted and changed the Learning Log to fit the various needs of the I-Search unit and students. We began with a shoe box. Our students kept their materials and reflections in the boxes and used them to write their papers. We liked the concept, but storage became cumbersome and the materials in the box had no organization which made it hard to find needed information. Next we folded several pieces of paper in half and stapled them together. We combined this with a manila envelope that was decorated. This worked fine but students were still having a hard time working with their information.

Presently, we use a Learning Log that grows with the research. It is made up of the responses, reflections, and work needed to complete the I-Search. The cover sheet (see Figure 1.8), along with each sheet that goes into the Learning Log, has three holes punched along the side. Brads or rings are used to hold the whole thing together. With this system, we are able to add, take away, and reorganize the log as needed. The three-hole punch system also allows students to place the brads in the holes that are not worn out. Extra brads need to be available for those students who are overly energetic in opening and closing. The Learning Log not only holds reflections about the learning that is taking place, but it also serves as a valuable resource for the information that will be needed for the project.

Our first two entries in the Learning Log are the Interest Map and the Possible I-Search Topics sheets. When the first two entries are made, they are stored in the classroom by groups. Storing the Learning Logs in groups allows for easy access and avoids the problem of being lost.

It is important to go through each Learning Log after the first section is complete. Check to see if students are on the right track and if they are beginning to think about meaningful topics that will carry them through the research. Respond to their work by encouraging

Figure 1.8

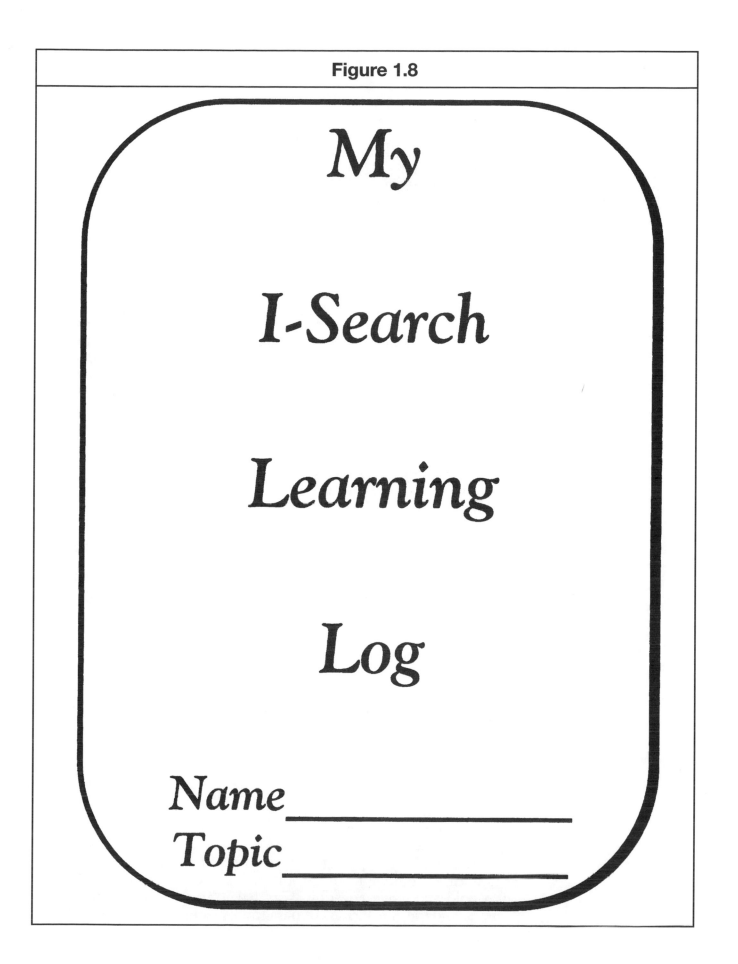

My

I-Search

Learning

Log

Name_____

Topic_____

and/or providing helpful suggestions. These suggestions can be written directly on the log or sticky notes may be used. Also, make note of any student that may need a preliminary conference to help get them on the right track.

SKIMMING AND SCANNING

Skimming and Scanning is another activity that evolved from listening to the needs of the students and from research about teaching for metacognitive reflection. In order for the students to make an informed and well-thought-out decision about their topic, they need the opportunity to explore various sources to get a feel for the subject. Joanna Cole, our model researcher, puts it best:

> For a science writer, it doesn't matter what the topic is, as long as it interests you. Because science isn't about what, it's about how and why. Let's say you are waiting for the bus, and you notice the leaves on the trees around you. You remember you have a school report due soon. Maybe it could be about leaves. How would I, Joanna, begin such a report? First, here's what I wouldn't do. I wouldn't decide right there at the bus stop what the report would say. I wouldn't go to the encyclopedia as soon as I got to school and start copying down information. I wouldn't make an outline. Some other writers might do these things successfully. But not me. First, I would read. (Cole, 1996: 23–24)

She goes on to explain how she would spread all her stuff (books, magazines, articles) on her bed and read in a very relaxing way. She would not worry about reading every word and would keep an open mind. She says she would not pick the first six facts that she found and write them down one after another without feeling a connection to her subject.

Adapted by permission of Joanna Cole with Wendy Saul: On the Bus with Joanna Cole: A Creative Biography. (Heinemann, A Division of Reed Elsevier Inc., Portsmouth, NH, 1992).

Before going to the library, read Chapter Four of Joanna Cole's book and discuss with students the importance of skimming and scanning resources and the opportunities it will give for learning and refining the I-Search topic. Encourage students to look at pictures, captions, and bold and italicized print. Also, have them read titles, topic sentences, and the conclusions of paragraphs from their sources.

LIBRARY SKILLS

Based on background experience and familiarity with the library, appropriate mini-lessons for this initial library trip should be arranged with the librarian. Sometimes the lessons consist of an introduction to the online catalog, a tour of where to find the information sources, the Dewey Decimal System, and the above-mentioned skimming and scanning. These lessons do not need to be lengthy but they do need to have enough information in them so that students will be able to find information on each one of their possible topics. The students are asked to search for sources on all three of their top choices. The library time is usually scheduled for an hour. This will allow a mini-lesson to be taught and then have the students search for resources. Students are asked to think of the answers to two questions while they are looking through the resources: Will there be enough information on the topic of my choice? Is the subject interesting?

The atmosphere in the library is relaxed, fun, and full of excitement. Students are sharing, talking, and absorbing a little about each one of their topics. This trip gives students the opportunity to make discoveries and become more responsible for their own learning. In fact, an important additional goal for this library trip is to build background knowledge on the topics. Building a base will help their research questions develop at a higher level and give them opportunities to ask questions they did not have prior to the trip to the library.

At the end of the first day, students reflect on their findings. This can be done on notebook paper and added to their Learning Log. Questions on which they reflect may include:

- Which topic had the most sources?
- Which topic seems to be of greatest interest to you?
- What will be my goal for tomorrow?

The Learning Logs are reviewed after the first library trip to evaluate where the students are and to help them with any problem areas. Some of these issues may be discussed the following day in a mini-lesson if most of the class would benefit. Lesson plans are developed in a way that allows for flexibility to follow the needs, issues, and interests of the students.

The following day is much like the day before. Students, however, are encouraged to review their Learning-Log reflections from the previous day. This will help them be more directed and goal oriented for the day's work.

At the conclusion of the second day, students will need to make a preliminary decision on their topic. On their Possible I-Search Topics sheets, students put a star by the topic they are most inclined to choose. Be sure to remind them to choose a topic based on the availability of sources, but most importantly on their interest.

The next step is to get the family involved. Parents/guardians should be informed and involved as early as possible. The family serves an important role and their support is greatly needed. The first step involves each student taking home the sheet titled "I-Search Topic Homework" (see Figure 1.9). After the final skim-and-scan library trip, students are given the homework for the evening. The homework involves students taking their top three choices home and sharing them with their family. The students need to share what was found in the library and discuss the suggestions and ideas with their family members. Based on the discussion, information availability, and interests, students are asked to make their decision. They fill out the paper, sign it, and then have their parent/guardian sign it. As the I-Search Homework sheets return, they are checked to make sure everyone is on the right track with their topic selection. Conferences are set up for those students who are still having trouble. The following story reflects the impact the family can have on the topic decision.

Mallory, a third grader, took her top three topics home. Her number-one choice was horses, number two was teaching, and number three was Washington D.C. Her family discussed her choices thoroughly. She had originally wanted to do Washington D.C. because each year her grandparents took one of the grandchildren to the capital on their annual trip. Mallory's turn would be the following year. She had not ranked it as number one because she was worried that our library did not have enough information. When she went home and talked it over with her family, she realized that she could interview all the family members who had made the trip and use a lot of the information they had brought back. She was excited to announce the next day that she had decided to do her I-Search on Washington D.C.

The following year when Mallory did make the trip to Washington D.C., she had a great time. Her mom reported that when Mallory would call to share her adventures, she talked so fast she was difficult to understand. Mallory returned from her trip to hand out patriotic gifts and to enthusiastically share her journey. Her I-Search the previous year had undoubtedly been a real-world learning experience that helped enrich her life and that of her family.

A great deal of time is spent choosing the topic. As a result of the time spent, students will have a topic that is meaningful and will carry them through the research. The next step is to begin reflecting and writing more on why the topic was chosen. This writing will serve

Figure 1.9

I-Search Topic Homework

1ˢᵗ — Take your first three topic choices home to share with your family.

2ⁿᵈ — Listen to and discuss the suggestions and ideas from your family members.

3ʳᵈ — Make a decision based on your interests and if you can find enough information to do a good research paper and project.

I have chosen to do my I-Search on _____.

Student _____

Parent _____

two purposes: Students will be able to internalize and then communicate their feelings about their topic while beginning the rough draft for their paper.

LESSON: WHY I CHOSE THIS TOPIC

MATERIALS NEEDED AND ADVANCE PREPARATION
- I-Search Learning Log
- Notebook paper or copy of "Why I Chose This Topic" sheet (see Figure 1.10)
- Transparency for writing teacher example of "Why I Chose This Topic"
- Overhead and transparency pens
- Think about and prepare the rough draft for "Why I Chose This Topic" for modeling

OBJECTIVE
Students will write their rough draft of the "Why I Chose This Topic" section of their I-Search paper.

ANTICIPATORY SET
- Before writing the "Why I Chose This Topic" rough draft of the I-Search paper, discuss the reasons for the choice. Begin by reading examples from past papers.

Wendi, a fifth grader, wrote:

> "I'm writing this paper because I went to San Antonio to Sea World two years ago. They had a show about Beluga whales and I thought they were unusual and neat. The melon was round and strange. A man was standing on it and the Beluga was picking him up and down. I thought it was interesting. When we started our I-Search I thought of all the neat things I saw. I thought of the Beluga." (Wendi Youngblood, 1995)

Matthew, a third grader, writes why he chose to do his I-Search on Go-Karts:

> "When I get a little older I can fix them and I can talk my parents into buying me one. I've been wanting to get one since my cousin Travis got one about four years ago. Now we go over on Birthday

Figure 1.10

Why I Chose This Topic

Sunday and drive it and go really fast. It seems like you're going the speed of light." (Matthew Beach, 1996)

Kari, a fourth grader, writes why she has chosen to research on horses:

"I chose to do my research on horses because I love horses and I wanted to know more about them. I haven't been on a horse since I was little. My aunt let my mom and I ride her horse one summer. I think it would be a whole lot of fun to ride horses. I also wanted to know how to take care of them. When I grow up I want to have a lot of horses. I think that horses are magnificent creatures and would consider them one of my most prized possessions." (Kari Lynch, 1999)

Samantha, a third grader, writes why she chose to research on Sea Otters.

"I chose this topic because, I think Sea Otters are cute. I care about them and I do not want to sit here and see them die. People have oil spills and let Sea Otters die. This topic is very exciting." (Samantha Lesikar, 1996)

CONNECTION

Explain to students that there are four sections to the I-Search paper. These include:

- Why I Chose This Topic
- What I Knew Before I Started My I-Search
- The Search
- What I Learned

Explain to students that they will be focusing on the "Why I Chose This Topic" portion of the I-Search paper.

GUIDED PRACTICE

- Discuss the reasons the above students chose their topics.
- Have students think of their own reasons for choosing their topics.
- Gather together in a circle on the floor.
- Go around the room and have the students share their topic and why they have chosen it. The teacher should model this first and then move around the circle encouraging the children to relate their topic choice to personal reasons.

Knowing the students helps during this activity. One student shared that he was doing his I-Search on comets. We asked him why and he said that he liked them. We reminded him of a trip he had taken this past summer. He realized where we were going with the question and went on to share his trip to NASA. He described some of the things that he saw and that he had been especially fascinated with the comet exhibits.

We are continuing to build our community of learners during this time together. As each child shares their topic and why they have chosen it, the others listen and ask questions. Even though we are all researching different topics, we are in this together. We have found that when we actually begin researching, everyone knows what the others are researching and are always willing to lend a hand. For example, one year a rambunctious third-grade boy was an avid reader and cautiously protected the two books he was able to check out from the library with each visit. A moment of celebration occurred the day he walked in from the library with his two books in hand. He dropped one off at his desk and took the other over to a girl who was doing her I-Search on Hawaii. He told her he had found the book in the library and knew she could use it for her research. Our community of learners was growing.

MODELING

- Model writing the first draft of "Why I Chose this Topic" after everyone shares their topics.
- Have students begin writing their rough drafts. Encourage them to just write and not to worry about spelling or punctuation (it will be edited and revised later).

CLOSURE

- As students finish their first drafts, they read over their writing and make any preliminary changes. Their first draft is then added to the learning logs for safe keeping.
- Discuss what was learned.

This chapter will help students with the first part of Step 1 of the Research Planner. We feel the extensive work done in this area is what will determine much of the success of the unit. Rather than jumping into the research, the students have had many opportunities to reflect, write, and think about their topic. In the next chapter we will work on the second part of Step 1 of the Research Planner: Students will begin developing questions for their research. We will also look at helping the students create a formal plan for the entire research process.

2 DEVELOPING QUESTIONS

In this chapter . . .
- What I Knew Before I Started My I-Search
- Lesson: What I Knew Before I Started My I-Search
- Higher-Level Questions
- Lesson: Higher-Level Questions
- Creating I-Search Questions
- Lesson: Creating I-Search Questions
- Organize and Make a Plan for Research
- Lesson: Make a Research Planner

"Students should feel proud that they have a question rather than pleased that they have the answer."

—Janice Szabos

Over the years, we have spent more and more time having students think about what they know about a topic and what it is they want to discover through their research. A very important goal is to help students create higher-level questions to enhance their thinking and reflection. "Asking questions, not just answering them, is a life support skill, maybe even a survival skill. It is connected to decision making and problem solving" (Johnson, 1995: 13). We have used different methods from leading educators to help students develop and use higher-level questions.

Most educators are familiar with the KWL chart. "It is reading strategy developed by Donna Ogle (1986). The K stands for What do you Know? W stands for What do you Want to know? And L is for What have you Learned?" (Fogarty, 1994: 80).

In *The Mindful School: How to Teach for Metacognitive Reflection*, Robin Fogarty explains that "through the process of sorting out what they already know about a topic, students are forced to call up prior knowledge and reorganize their thoughts and connections about it. Then, based on facts they already have in the forefront of their minds, students can proceed to focus on other aspects of the topic that they are wondering about or want to know more about" (Fogarty, 1994: 80–81).

The organization of the I-Search paper is very similar to the KWL chart. "Why I Chose this Topic" sets the purpose for learning. "What I Knew Before I Started My I-Search" helps students "make meaning of new facts in relationship to what they already know and want to know" (Fogarty, 1994: 81). The development of the questions and

"The Search" helps students organize what they want to know and where to find it. Finally, the "What I Learned" section is identical in both the I-Search paper and the KWL chart. This reiterates our belief that the I-Search process is a metacognitive process for students to work through.

As a result of the metacognition involved in the I-Search process, the next step is for students to work through what they already know about their topic. Fogarty explains that even if students write obvious misconceptions, it is important to record them. The students' thinking needs to be visible and later, as the subject is explored in more depth, the students will begin to make the necessary corrections (Fogarty, 1994).

Emily Cleveland, a fifth grader, is a powerful example of making her thinking visible. She writes:

I chose cancer because my aunt died of it when I was in the third grade. I want to know more about how it kills people and how cancer forms. I want to know if you can catch cancer like a cold or you have to be a certain person in a certain climate. I also want to know if there is a way to cure cancer. Finally, I want to know what makes cancer spread to other parts of your body. Does it start in your stomach, head, or lungs? (Emily Cleveland, 1998)

Emily's topic was very important to her and had obviously been on her mind for several years. She had some very serious questions regarding the subject. She was able to clear up her misconceptions when she began researching. It was a very informative and meaningful project for her.

WHAT I KNEW BEFORE I STARTED MY I-SEARCH

We help students work through this part of the I-Search paper at this point for three reasons. First, it will help them when they get ready to develop their questions. Second, creating the rough draft now will avoid the problem of having to sort out what was known before the research and what was learned after the research. Third, when students begin researching they will be constructing meaning from facts they already know.

Figure 2.1

What I Knew Before I Started My I-Search

LESSON: WHAT I KNEW BEFORE I STARTED MY I-SEARCH

MATERIALS AND ADVANCE PREPARATION
- Transparency of "What I Knew Before I Started My I-Search"
- Notebook paper or copies of "What I Knew Before I Started My I-Search" for each student (See Figure 2.1).
- Overhead projector and overhead pens
- Teacher prepares what is known about his/her topic

OBJECTIVE
Students will write their rough drafts of "What I Knew Before I Started My I-Search."

ANTICIPATORY SET
- Read several examples of the "What I Knew Before I Started My I-Search" section. The following are some student examples:

Subject: Washington DC

"I know that the president lives in the White House. I also know that Washington D.C. is our nation's capitol. I know that there are good places to eat like Hard Rock Café and Planet Hollywood. I also know that the president has to do lots of work in Washington D.C."

Mallory Levy, 3rd grade (1997)

Subject: Trains

"Before I started my I-Search I knew trains were big and powerful. They could pull over 500,000 tons. The engine of the train is in the back. I also knew they have funny looking wheels. I wanted to find out how they get so powerful and what it looks like inside I also wanted to find out how long they could get."

Jeremy Holmsly, 3rd grade (1996)

Subject: Michael Jordan

"Before I started my I-Search about Michael Jordan I knew that he was the best basketball player to ever live. I knew Michael was cut from his high school basketball team. I also knew that he won six championships and he has six MVP awards in the championships. Michael retired from basketball in 1999 and his number was retired. His number is 23. I knew that his sophomore, junior, and senior year in high school he played for Lanley High. I knew Michael played for North Carolina College. His college number 23 was also retired. In 1995 he retired to play baseball. He played with a minor league team. Then he came back to the NBA."

Riley Dodge, 4th grade (1999)

- Discuss the above examples with the students. Explain that, by sorting out what they know about a topic before they begin researching, they will be able to develop better questions and see their progress after they are finished researching.

INPUT AND MODELING

- Model the rough draft of "What I Knew Before I Started My I-Search" . . . —read and think aloud while writing.

GUIDED PRACTICE

- Ask students to think about what they already know about their subject. They can pull from prior knowledge and background information that was gained from skimming and scanning.
- Have students turn to their neighbors in the classroom and discuss what they know right now about their topics.

INDEPENDENT PRACTICE

- Have students begin writing their rough drafts while the monitoring.

CLOSURE

- Have students read over their rough drafts and make any preliminary changes.
- Have students add their rough drafts to their Learning Logs.
- Discuss what was learned.

HIGHER-LEVEL QUESTIONS

We use an activity found in Fogarty's *The Mindful School: How to Teach for Metacognitive Reflection* to help students become comfortable with creating higher-level questions. Fogarty explains that the concept of fat and skinny questions is based on Bloom's Taxonomy of Higher-Order Thinking. "Simply, the fat questions call for elaborated answers, full of examples and details; while skinny questions demand to-the-point answers that often require short and yes or no responses" (Fogarty, 1994: 30). We usually do the following higher-order question activity with students prior to the I-Search because of other research projects and questioning strategies we use in class. If students have not been exposed to this concept, however, this is the time to do it. The following is a slightly modified version of Fogarty's Higher-Order Question Lesson.

LESSON: HIGHER-LEVEL QUESTIONS

MATERIALS NEEDED AND ADVANCE PREPARATION
- Science or social studies textbooks for each student
- Chart paper
- Markers in different colors
- Draw a T-chart for "Big" and "Little" questions (see Figure 2.2).

OBJECTIVE
Students will learn how to generate higher-level questions for their I-Search.

ANTICIPATORY SET AND MODELING
Begin the activity by introducing the difference between big (fat) and little (skinny) questions. Most often, little questions begin with words like "what," "where," "who," and "when," while big questions might begin with "why" or "how." Students can practice identifying these types of questions by studying the questions at the end of chapters in textbooks. Examples of little questions include:

- Who is the author?
- What is the title of the chapter?

Figure 2.2	
Interview Activity	
Big Questions	**Little Questions**

Examples of big questions include:

- How might you explain the stages of the moon?
- Why do you think that?

GUIDED PRACTICE
- Practice generating and discriminating between big and little questions with the class by asking a student volunteer to be interviewed. Use a T-chart to record the questions under the proper heading: big or little.
- Explain to students that big questions usually require a "bigger," more thought out answer. Typically these questions begin with "why" or "how," but not always.
- Have a student ask the volunteer a question. After the question is asked, have the volunteer answer the question. Based on how the question was asked and how it was answered, have students decide if it was a big question or a little question. Record the question in the proper section of the T-chart.
- Repeat the above process for several more questions.

INPUT AND REFLECTION
After four or five questions, ask students the following

- How does someone answer a big question?
- How does someone answer a little question?
- When do you learn the most about a person answering a question?
- If you had to conduct an interview, which questions would give the most information for you to use—big or little?

CLOSURE
- Ask students to think about the difference between big and little questions. Think about some examples of each.
- Have students share their thoughts with their neighbor.
- Discuss as a class. Call on several students to share their thoughts.

This activity is adapted from the strategy on page 33 of The Mindful School: How to Teach for Metacognitive Reflection *by Robin Fogarty © 1994 by IRI/Skylight Training and Publishing, Inc. by permission of Skylight Training and Publishing Inc., Arlington Heights, IL.*

CREATING I-SEARCH QUESTIONS

The previous lesson helps students practice and reflect on big and little questions. They will be able to feel more comfortable creating their own big questions as they are exposed to and have practice creating class and individual questions throughout the year.

The KWL connection helped us realize that merely evaluating what is already known and what you want to find out about a topic helps with developing questions. The previously mentioned skimming-and-scanning technique also helps students develop higher-level questions by helping them to build their background knowledge. We also found that teaching the difference between lower-level and higher-level questions helped students with their thinking, especially when integrated throughout the disciplines and the school day. Lastly, we use the "Question Chart" to help students with creating their research questions (see Figure 2.3). The following is a suggested lesson on how to use the Question Chart when facilitating the development of each student's individual I-Search questions.

Figure 2.3

QUESTION CHART

Name _____ Topic _____

What I Want to Know	My Research Questions

LESSON: CREATING I-SEARCH QUESTIONS

MATERIALS AND ADVANCE PREPARATION
- Transparency of Question Chart (Figure 2.3)
- Overhead pens in different colors
- Prepared Question Chart for modeling
- Overhead projector.

OBJECTIVE
Students will utilize their skills developing higher- and lower-level questions when creating their own I-Search questions.

ANTICIPATORY SET AND INTRODUCTION
Explain to students that good researchers research with a purpose. They search for the answers to questions that they have. Tell students that they are becoming good researchers and today they will create their questions for their own research.

CONNECTION AND INPUT
Direct students into a discussion on big and little questions. Review the differences between the two.

MODELING
- Show a blank Question Chart on the overhead.
- Brainstorm in think-aloud fashion "what I want to know" about the topic. List only the keywords ("treasure words").

Note: refer to Chapter 4 for more on treasure words.

INDEPENDENT PRACTICE
- Pass out a blank Question Chart to each student.
- Have students list the things they want to find out about their topic. Remind them to refer to the time they skimmed and scanned and discovered things they wanted to know more about. Encourage them to brainstorm and use keywords on their lists.
- Have students share their lists with their partners and make needed corrections.
- Monitor the students.

Figure 2.4

QUESTION CHART

Name _____ Topic _____

who, what, when, where, (why, how)

What I Want to Know	My Research Questions
• exact location? ✗	1. Where is Lake Tahoe located?
• cost of trip? ✗	2. How much would it cost to get to Lake Tahoe?
• (entertainment?) ✗	3. Where is the best and most affordable place to stay? Why?
• [best place to stay?] ✗	4. What are the tourist attractions and entertainment?
• (tourist attractions?) ✗	5. How did Lake Tahoe become a resort?
• history? ✗	6. Other interesting information?
• [cost of lodging?] ✗	
• dress? ✗	

Adapted from Marilyn Joyce and Julie Tallman's "PreNotetaking Sheet," from Making the Writing and Research Connection with the I-Search Process. *Copyright by Neal-Schuman Publishers, Inc.*

MODELING WITH INDEPENDENT PRACTICE

The next activity requires students to group items that go together. The purpose of this activity is to put similar questions together so that research questions will not be repeated.

- Show students the model Question Chart (teacher's chart).
- Read over the list and put a star by those things that are of most interest.
- Have students repeat the above process.
- Read over the list and draw an oval around those things that go together.
- Monitor students as they repeat the above process.
- Put a rectangle around those things that go together.
- Monitor students as they repeat the process.
- Put a dotted oval around additional things that go together.
- Monitor students as they repeat the process, if needed.

(See Figure 2.4 for an example of a completed Question Chart.)

MODELING WITH GUIDED PRACTICE

- At the top of the Question Sheet, list "Who, What, Where, When, Why and How." Circle the "Why" and "How" because those words lend themselves to higher-level questions. Students then repeat the above process on their Question Chart.
- Take the first item from the first column and, in the second column, model turning it into a formal research question. Also, model how to combine items that go together from the first column. Model developing two research questions and then have the students try one.

Note: Explain to students that developing higher-level questions will make their research better. Many times they only need to add the words "Why" or "How" to make it a higher-level question. Sometimes, however, it is important to create a little question because higher-level questions can build on them.

- As students finish, have them share. Check to see if everyone is on the right track and understands the process. Model developing the rest of the questions and then have them do the same. Slow the process down if they are struggling.
- The last research question should be "other interesting information." This will allow students to add interesting information to their project for which they didn't realize they had a question.

CLOSURE
- Have students share their questions with one another.
- Call on several students to share their questions. Ask the class if the questions are big or little.
- Have students add the Question Chart to their I-Search Learning Log.

Review the students' Question Charts to assess their work and make sure everyone is on the right track. Set up time to conference with those who are struggling. If there is a similar problem with a majority of the students' Question Charts, develop a quick mini-lesson to clear up the problem.

Choosing a topic and developing questions are extremely important components of the I-Search. Teachers and librarians need to devote time to help students develop well-thought-out topics and questions so that the research will be more successful. Dedicating the time and effort to this preliminary work will prove to be more favorable than one day announcing to the students that they will be going to the library to do research. When research is done that way, students have no direction and valuable library and research time can be wasted. The opportunity for students to connect to a subject, to ask good questions, and to be involved in a community of enthusiastic learners may also be missed. Take the time to get started in a comprehensive and meaningful way. It is worth it!

ORGANIZE AND MAKE A PLAN FOR RESEARCH

Students are ready to develop their research plan when they have completed this preliminary work. The Research Planner (Figure 1.2) is a guide that follows five steps to research. It is an organized plan of action that students can use to map out their research. Ideally, once students have chosen their topic and developed their questions, they can fill out steps one through five of the Research Planner. If students have not used the planner, they may be introduced to it during the I-Search process. In fact, this book is organized as if your students have not been exposed to an information organizer. Students can learn the Research Planner while they work through the I-Search process. However, students need to see a general plan for the research in the beginning. This will help set a meaningful purpose for the learning. The following is a lesson that will help expose students to the plan. This will enable them to add and revise along the way.

LESSON: MAKE A RESEARCH PLANNER

MATERIALS NEEDED AND ADVANCE PREPARATION
- Blank transparencies or chart paper
- Two sheets of notebook paper for each student
- Markers or overhead pens

OBJECTIVE
Students will make a plan for their research.

ANTICIPATORY SET AND INTRODUCTION
- Compare the Research Planner to going on a family vacation. Not many people wake up one morning, decide to go on a trip, pile the family in the car, and take off. This type of trip would not be very successful. It is important for the family to sit down and decide where to go, how to get there, and what needs to be done to prepare. The family will also assess the success of the trip along the way and when they return home.
- Explain to the students that they have begun a very important research project and that planning out the research will help them to know where the research is going, what will be expected, and how they will know they are doing a good job. The research trip will be more fun, meaningful, and successful if there is a plan.

MODELING AND GUIDED PRACTICE
- Pass out two pieces of notebook paper for each student.
- Use two blank transparencies or two sheets of large chart paper.
- On the first page, center the title "Research Planner." Students repeat.
- On the first line, write "What Do I Want to Know?" Students repeat.
- Skip down to the middle of the page and write, "Where Can I Find the Answers?" Students repeat.
- At the top of page two, write "How Will I Record the Information That I Find?" Students repeat.
- Skip down a third of the way and write, "How Will I Show What I Learned?" Students repeat.
- Skip down three-fourths of the way and write, "How Will I Know I Did a Good Job?" Students repeat.

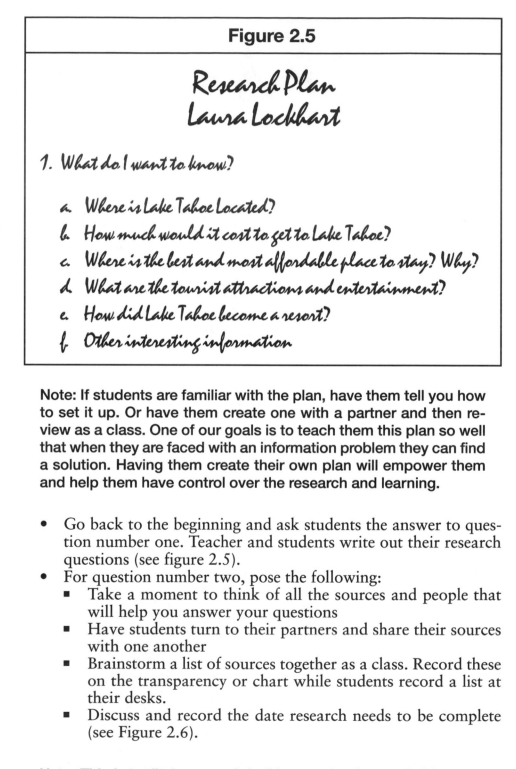

Figure 2.5

Research Plan
Laura Lockhart

1. What do I want to know?

  a. Where is Lake Tahoe Located?
  b. How much would it cost to get to Lake Tahoe?
  c. Where is the best and most affordable place to stay? Why?
  d. What are the tourist attractions and entertainment?
  e. How did Lake Tahoe become a resort?
  f. Other interesting information

Note: If students are familiar with the plan, have them tell you how to set it up. Or have them create one with a partner and then review as a class. One of our goals is to teach them this plan so well that when they are faced with an information problem they can find a solution. Having them create their own plan will empower them and help them have control over the research and learning.

- Go back to the beginning and ask students the answer to question number one. Teacher and students write out their research questions (see figure 2.5).
- For question number two, pose the following:
  - Take a moment to think of all the sources and people that will help you answer your questions
  - Have students turn to their partners and share their sources with one another
  - Brainstorm a list of sources together as a class. Record these on the transparency or chart while students record a list at their desks.
  - Discuss and record the date research needs to be complete (see Figure 2.6).

Note: This is preliminary work in this area. In chapter 3 this question will be explored in more detail.

Figure 2.6

---

2. Where can I find the answers?
Internet
Encyclopedia
Phone calls
Books
School library
Public library
Librarian

Research completed by 4-20-99

- Ask how we will record the information that we find. Possible answers could be notebook paper, note cards, or note sheets. Note Sheets are explained in more detail in Chapter 4. Record the answer on the chart while students fill in their planner (see Figure 2.7).
- Ask how you will show what you learned. Everyone will be doing an I-Search paper and presentation, record these as "a" and "b." For "c," students will be choosing their own project. As a class, brainstorm all the possible projects students could do to show what they have learned (see Figure 2.8). See Chapter 7 for more on projects.
- Discuss and record the due date for the paper, project, and oral presentation.

Note: The teacher may want to use a sign-up sheet for the oral presentation.

Figure 2.7

---

3. How will I record the information that I find?
A Note Sheet will be used for each research question to record the information and cite sources.

Figure 2.8

---

4. How can I show what I learned?
   a. I-Search Paper—due 4-28-99
   b. Presentation—due 5-10-99
   c. Puppet Show—due 5-10-99

Note: Students need to make a commitment to a project at this time; however, they may change their minds later. Students may be in the middle of their research and decide on a better way to show what they have learned. The important thing is for students to know and understand where their research is going.

- Ask how we will know we have done a good job.
  The teachers and students together will create a checklist to assess and evaluate the project. Help students create five to six criteria for credit (see Figure 2.9).

CLOSURE

Ask how the Research Planner will help us with our research journey.

- Have students think about this first.
- Then have students share with a partner.
- Discuss as a class.
- Add the Research Planner to their I-Search Learning Log.

Figure 2.9

---

5. How will I know I did a good job?
   ___ Did I answer all my research questions?
   ___ Did I use the best sources?
   ___ Did I give credit to my sources?
   ___ Did I show my learning with the paper, project, and presentation?
   ___ Did I do my best and neatest work?

This book is organized by the Research Planner format. As mentioned before, students can be introduced to the process one step at a time; however, we feel it is important that all students have a general introduction to the plan in the beginning. This will help them connect their learning and begin with the end in mind.

SECTION II:

WHERE CAN I FIND THE ANSWERS TO MY QUESTIONS?

Chapter 3: Finding Sources and Experts

3 FINDING SOURCES AND EXPERTS

In this chapter...

- Brainstorm Sources
- Interviews
- Lesson: Conducting an Interview

"Knowing how to find the answer to a question is in essence the best part of learning."

Anonymous

Guiding students through the never-ending maze of information is challenging. Students need the opportunity to learn what is out there and how to access it. We can no longer teach them everything; we must teach them how to find the information they need. According to Peter Cochrane in *Tips for Time Travelers*, "mankind's knowledge is now doubling in a period of less than two years" (Pritchett, 1999: 13). With this in mind we need to prepare students to deal effectively with this enormous wealth of information that can become unmanageable even to the experts. In this chapter, we will discuss various strategies and techniques that will help students move through the overwhelming variety of sources to find answers to their questions.

BRAINSTORM SOURCES

Step 2 of the Research Planner focuses on where the answers to the questions can be found. This section will become more sophisticated as students become more familiar and confident information problem solvers. They can, however, be guided through this activity to expose them to many different possibilities. The goal is to get them thinking about all the different choices that they have, get them to evaluate those choices, and then to decide on the best ones for their research. The following activity is an extension to the work that has already been done with the Research Planner.

Step One: Explain to students that they will be helping one another with sources for their I-Search. Arrange students in a circle on the floor or at their desks. Each student should still have their Research Planner.

Step Two: Students will take turns sharing their topic with the group. Others in the group will provide suggestions about where they can find information. These suggestions may include specific books, software, articles, Websites, people, and places to contact. As students listen to the suggestions, have them record the information under Step 2 of their Research Planner. Move around the circle so that everyone has a chance to share. (This step may be broken into two sessions.)

Note: A variation of this activity is to have the students write down their name and topic on a sheet of paper. Students then pass their papers around the room and other students jot possible sources and experts on the papers as they come by.

Step Three: Have students look at their list of possible sources and put a star or highlight those sources they feel would be of greatest benefit to them (see Figure 3.1). As students finish, pose the following question: What did you learn today that will help you with your I-Search?

The above activity will move your class one more step toward building a community of learners. The foundation for this community is laid by students having chances to help others with their topics while gaining information that may be useful to their own searches.

Each year we are amazed at the amount of information that our students provide one another. We have had many students offer their relatives as possible people to interview, bring books and articles from home to help someone with their search, suggest Websites as sources, and pick up information for one another.

Figure 3.1

2. Where can I find the answers?
   Internet
   Encyclopedia
   Brochures
   Phone calls
   Travel agency
   Books
   School library
   Public library
   Interview relatives who have been there
   Librarian

INTERVIEWS

As a part of the above activity, people will often come up as possible sources. As a result, students need to be aware of the proper ways to conduct an interview. Teaching interviewing skills will help students practice creating higher-level questions, give them opportunities to participate in cooperative learning activities, and help them with focusing and summarizing information while teaching them the etiquette of interviewing (see Figure 3.2). The following activity can be used during the I-Search unit or in isolation. The activity should take two or three days to complete. Modify it as needed.

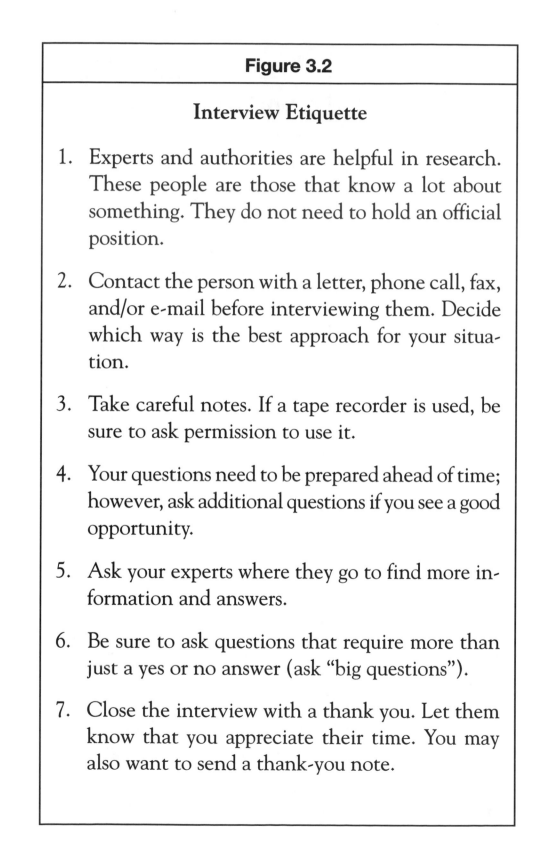

Figure 3.2

Interview Etiquette

1. Experts and authorities are helpful in research. These people are those that know a lot about something. They do not need to hold an official position.

2. Contact the person with a letter, phone call, fax, and/or e-mail before interviewing them. Decide which way is the best approach for your situation.

3. Take careful notes. If a tape recorder is used, be sure to ask permission to use it.

4. Your questions need to be prepared ahead of time; however, ask additional questions if you see a good opportunity.

5. Ask your experts where they go to find more information and answers.

6. Be sure to ask questions that require more than just a yes or no answer (ask "big questions").

7. Close the interview with a thank you. Let them know that you appreciate their time. You may also want to send a thank-you note.

LESSON: CONDUCTING AN INTERVIEW

MATERIALS AND ADVANCE PREPARATION
- Three half-sheets of paper of three different colors for each student
- Video recording of someone conducting an interview
- Example written interview to show students (an interview of a significant other or friend will work)
- Transparencies of the model interview
- Overhead projector
- Interview etiquette handout for each student (Figure 3.3)
- Transparency of the reflection questions
- Joanna Cole's autobiography

OBJECTIVE
Students will learn how to conduct an interview, focus, and summarize information into a story.

ANTICIPATORY SET AND INTRODUCTION
- Review the work done for Step Two of the Research Planner. Remind students that, during the brainstorm of possible sources, people were mentioned quite a bit. Review past I-Searches for connections: Who did Kevin interview in his paper "The Inside and Outside of a Diesel Truck"? Who did Avril interview in the article "The Ring of Truth"?
- Joanna Cole can be used as a real-world connection to seeking outside sources for research. In Chapter Three of her autobiography, she describes the importance of finding an expert to help her write her books. She describes a time when she was writing a book on snakes and needed to talk to a herpetologist. She describes how she contacted such a scientist and her experience interviewing him. She concludes the section by stating "I know that I am not a scientist; I am a science writer, which is quite different. My job is to try to understand scientists' complex ideas and to communicate them in a way that makes sense to my readers" (Cole, 1996:21).

  This statement reiterates the importance of seeking out the answers to our questions and being able to communicate the information in a way that makes sense to our audiences.

REFLECTION

- Post the following questions: "Why does Joanna Cole use interviews?" "Why does she feel interviews are important?" Have students think about the answers to these two questions and then share their thoughts with a neighbor.

CONNECTION AND INPUT

Tell students that since they may be conducting interviews for their I-Searches it will be important to review the criteria of a good interview (Figure 3.2). Give students a copy of the criteria so they can highlight information and take additional notes. Review and briefly discuss each one.

MODELING

- To enable students to observe a good interview, use a two- to three-minute video displaying a person asking questions and the interviewee answering. Another variation is to ask another teacher or student to model a good interview. Before showing the video or conducting the interview, ask students to make sure they observe what each person does during the interview and what types of questions are asked.
- After the video clip or role playing session, ask students the following questions:
  - Who did most of the talking?
  - Why is it important for the person being interviewed to do most of the talking?
  - What types of question did the person conducting the interview ask?

(Be sure to discuss big questions—those that elicit a longer response.)

GUIDED PRACTICE AND MODELING

- Pass out the three different-colored half-sheets of paper to each student.
- Make sure each student has a partner.

Note: Each step below should be modeled by the teacher first.

- Have students fold two of the pieces of paper in half. Next, number the cards as shown in Figure 3.3.
- In Section 1, have students write down four questions they would like to ask their partner. Encourage students to use big questions so that they will get as much information as possible.

Figure 3.3 Numbered Question Cards

1.	2.	3.	4.	5.

- Have students ask their partners the four questions from Section 1. Students should record their answers using "treasure words" in Section 2 (see Chapter 4 for more on "treasure words").
- Have students look over the answers to the questions that they asked. Pose the following questions: "What is on the card that interested you?" "What do you want to know more about?" Make a decision and come up with four more big questions that focus on that one thing and have students enter them in Section 3.
- Students will then need to ask their partners these new questions and record the answers in Section 4.
- Next, students will take the information that they have collected and develop it into a story that would help a reader get to know the person they interviewed. This story should be written on Section 5 of the card. Remind students to focus the story so they will keep the reader's attention (see Figure 3.4 for completed interview).
- Have students read their first draft to their partners. The partner will need to verify that all the information is correct. Next, students will need to revise and edit their draft to make it more clear.

INDEPENDENT PRACTICE
- Students can publish their stories in many ways. Possibilities include a small picture book, an article, or a poster.

CLOSURE
- Post the following question on chart paper: "What makes a good interview?" Students share their thoughts while you record the information. Post the chart in the classroom.
- Share with students that they will use the skills they learned to-

Figure 3.4 Numbered Questions Cards

1.
- What's your favorite sport? Why?
- What's your best memory as a child?
- What do you like to do in your spare time?
- What was your favorite pet? Why?

2
- basketball, golf, — enjoy it, relaxing, healthy, fun
- playing golf, had good time, played at Willow Springs — on golf team
- spend time with family, play golf
- Tiger, did everything together, had him 5 years, cried when he died

3.
- What kinds of things did you do with Tiger?
- What did Tiger look like?
- How old were you when you had Tiger?
- What was a good memory you have about Tiger? (Funniest)

4.
- used to go in woods and look for stuff, companion, looked out for me
- Beagle, brown, black, white, still like Beagles today
- little bitty kid — ages 4 to 10
- When he was eating, better leave him alone. First messed with him and learned lesson. Would walk outside while he was eating, accidently bump into him — he would growl I'd just say "be quiet Tiger"

5.

"I was a little bitty kid", said Jordan, "and Tiger would look after me. The only thing was, you better not mess with him when he was eating."

Tiger was Jordan's dog for six years. They used to go in the woods and look for stuff. Jordan says that Tiger was a great companion and a great dog. Except, of course, for his stingy eating habits. To this day, when Jordan sees a Beagle he thinks of Tiger and what a good friend he was.

day to conduct interviews for their I-Search projects. Pass out an interview sheet to each student (see Figure 3.5). They may record their research questions on the sheet and take them home so they will be ready for an interview.

Note: Home connection: Send a note home updating parents/guardians on the activities and learning being done. Elicit their help in setting up interviews

Interview lesson adapted by permission of Linda Rief: Seeking Diversity: Language Arts With Adolescents *(Heinemann, A division of Reed Elsevier, Inc. Portsmouth, NH, 1992).*

Figure 3.5

Interview

Name of Person Interviewed _____

Title _____

Date of Interview _____

Person Conducting the Interview _____

Questions:

1.

2.

3.

4.

5.

6.

When you are through with your interview, bring this sheet, with the answers, to school.

The above activity helps our community of learners grow by helping students support one another. They learn about the person they are interviewing, and publishing the stories helps them get to know others.

We usually do not require that the students conduct an interview for their I-Search project; however, we strongly urge the students and their parents/guardians to try and set up an interview. Students benefit greatly from learning how to do interviews and having the experience of actually conducting one.

In the past, students have used these skills to interview many different people for their I-Search. The following is a list of interviews that third, fourth, and fifth graders have conducted:

Topic: Cats—interviewed the family veterinarian

Topic: Soccer—faxed a local professional soccer team

Topic: Diesel trucks—interviewed neighbor who owned a diesel truck

Topic: Trains—interviewed a retired train engineer (as a result of his interview, this child was able to borrow materials including a model train, communication light, and a conductor's jacket to share in his presentation)

Topic: Hawaii—interviewed a teacher from down the hall who had recently returned from a vacation in Hawaii

Topic: Washington D.C.—interviewed family members who had been to Washington D.C.

Topic: Why do children take drugs?—interviewed older sister's friends that were in high school

Topic: Grooming dogs—interviewed the people who groomed his dog

Learning how to find the answers to questions is a very important skill. This skill is not one that can be discussed in only one chapter. Locating sources are skills that are integrated throughout the I-Search. As a result, students will be exposed to research skills in the beginning (skimming and scanning), towards the middle (this chapter), and towards the end of the I-Search (when they go to the library to research their topic—Chapter 5).

SECTION III:

HOW WILL I RECORD THE INFORMATION THAT I FIND?

4 TAKING NOTES AND CITING SOURCES

In this chapter...

- Lesson: Notetaking and Citing Sources

Copying from the encyclopedia or other sources is common practice for many researchers no matter what their age. Today's age of information makes it imperative that students be able to locate information, use the information, and give credit to their sources. "Reading for specific information and taking notes may be the most challenging step in the information problem-solving process. Students need many developmentally appropriate opportunities to locate and use information before mastering the technique" (Jansen, 1996). The I-Search project is authentic and students are working with actual researchable questions. These components help the I-Search to be meaningful and real world for students as they learn notetaking skills.

We believe it is never too early to teach students the important skills of notetaking and citing sources. Through innovative work by teachers and librarians, we have found that the task is possible. Students learn quickly the importance of not copying word-for-word from their sources. They also learn to synthesize the information into their own words and to give credit to their sources.

We use a term called "treasure words" to teach notetaking skills. This term was created by Barbara Jansen, a Texas librarian and curriculum specialist. She says that: "more than just extracting needed information, notetaking consists of three steps: identification of keywords and related work in the researchable question, skimming and scanning, and extracting needed information. The steps begin after students have defined and narrowed the task, constructed researchable questions, and located appropriate sources" (Jansen, 1996: 29).

We also utilize the work of Corene Madely, a second-grade teacher in Troy, Texas. Madely developed a method for taking notes while she was teaching a research unit on "Christmas Around the World." She found that her students needed a method to organize their information and enough space to write. She developed the Note Sheet to help her students do this (see Figure 4.1).

A Note Sheet is used for each research question. Students write their question at the top and record their notes in the first section. Their source is cited beside the information. There is room for another source on the same page. Additional sheets may be used for the same ques-

Figure 4.1

Note Sheet

Name_____   **Topic** _____

Question

Notes	Source

p.

Notes	Source

p.

Summary

tion if students have more than two sources. Students could simply staple all relevant Note Sheets together (this will be discussed further later in the chapter).

The following lesson shows how to teach notetaking skills and cite sources using the Note Sheet. It may take between one and two days to complete the lesson.

LESSON: NOTETAKING AND CITING SOURCES

MATERIALS NEEDED

- Transparency of a treasure map or a large treasure map
- Transparency of blank Note Sheet
- Copies of blank Note Sheets for each student
- Overhead pens
- Prepared research question from teacher's or previous student's research
- Two different transparencies of encyclopedia, reference book, or Internet article—make sure the two articles answer the question in different ways
- Copies of second article for each student
- Overhead projector and pens
- Student copies of "How to Cite Your Source" information sheet (see Figure 4.2).

OBJECTIVE

Students will learn how to take notes and cite their sources using the Note Sheet.

INTRODUCTION

Explain to students that as researchers they will be faced with numerous sources and information. There will be a need to record and organize this information so that they will be able to use it when they make their projects and write their papers.

ANTICIPATORY SET

"Relate notetaking to a pirate's treasure map. The map itself is like the article or chapter of a book containing information about the topic. The "X" on the map, which marks the exact location of the buried treasure, is the section of the text that contains the needed informa-

---

Figure 4.2

How to Cite Your Source

BOOKS—
Author (last name, first name). Title (underlined), publisher, copyright date, page number.

> Example: Goodman, Billy. The Rainforest, Beasy Pub., 1996, p.56.

MAGAZINES—
Author of Article (last name, first name). Title of Article (in quotations), Title of Magazine (underlined), page number, date.

> Example: Johnson, Dave. "The Orbit of the Earth," Zoo Books, p. 89, June 1988.

ENCYCLOPEDIA—
Author of Article (last name, first name). Title of Article (in quotations), Name of Encyclopedia (underlined), page number, copyright date.

> Example: Martin, John. "Turtle," Academic American Encyclopedia, p. 23, 25–27, 1985.

INTERVIEW—
Name of Person interviewed (last name, first name). Title, the word Interview, date of interview.

> Example: McAnns, Chris. Veterinarian, Interview, April 12, 1999.

CD-ROM program—
Author (last name, first name). Year (in parenthesis). Title of CD Program (in quotations), type of medium.

> Example: Clay, Ron. (1997). "George Washington," CD-ROM.

VIDEO—
Producer (last name, first name). Year (in parenthesis). Title of Video (in quotations), Name of Production Company. Length of Video.

> Example: Barr, Casey. (1999). "Oasis Production," ABC Productions. 55 minutes.

ELECTRONIC MAIL—
Author (last name, first name). Year, Month, Day (in parenthesis). Subject (E-mail to name of recipient (in parenthesis), Type of Medium (in parenthesis), how to retrieve.

> Example: Sweeny, Gary. (1999, August, 1). Oceans (E-mail to Taylor Jones), (Online), Tjones@osuv.edu.

INTERNET—
Author (last name, first name). Year of Publication (in parenthesis). Title of Publication. Type of Medium (in parenthesis). Available: Web address. Access date (in parenthesis).

> Example: Jones, Sarah. (1998). Water Polo. (Online). Available: www.waterpolo.com. (June 14, 1999).

tion, or "answer" for a specific research question. A pirate must dig for the treasure chest, tossing aside dirt, weeds, and rocks—trash. A researcher must dig to find words that help him answer the questions—treasure words. He or she must "toss aside" unnecessary sentences, phrases, and words—trash words. These words are not trash to the original source, only to the researcher because they do not answer the research questions" (Jansen, 1994: 30).

INPUT AND MODELING

- Pass out a blank Note Sheet to each student
- Show the Note Sheet with a prepared question (students are encouraged to take notes of what the teacher is doing on the overhead).
- Keywords are underlined from the question. Related words are listed underneath the question. These keywords and related words will help students when they begin scanning the article to find the answer to the questions. Model underlining the keywords, listing related words, and looking up keywords in a thesaurus to find additional related words. (There will be more on keywords in Chapter 5.)
- Describe to students how the article was found. For example, I went to the library and searched the online catalog under the subject heading "Lake Tahoe." The catalog listed a reference book and I wrote down the shelf number. When I found the book, I turned to the index. I looked for the word *resort* to find information on vacation resorts. Then I turned to the appropriate page and found this article. This example reiterates how to locate and access appropriate sources.
- Put the article on the overhead and scan the article until the right heading is located.
- Put your finger at the end of the first sentence and then read it. Think aloud: "Does this sentence answer my question?"
- If the answer is "no," tell the students that the sentence is trash to them. Go on to the next sentence and put your finger at the end.
- If the answer is "yes," read that sentence again word-by-word. Think aloud: "Which words are needed to answer the question?" The words that answer the question are the treasure words. Those that do not answer the question are trash words.
- Write the treasure words in the "note" section of the Note Sheet. Count the words in the sentence used and then the words in the "note" section of the Note Sheet. Think aloud: "Wow, there were 15 words in the sentence and I only had to write 4 words for my notes. I saved space and time."

- Inform students that it is very important to give credit to their sources. Relate this issue to borrowing by sharing the following story: Pretend you would like to ride your friend's bike. It is against the law to go to his house and take the bike. That is called stealing. It is, however, OK to borrow the bike if you ask your friend. The same goes for words. It is against the law to steal someone's words. That is called plagiarism. However, if you borrow their words and give them credit for using them, then it is OK.
- Demonstrate how to cite the source. The information required is up to the teacher. We usually require the minimum amount of information with beginning researchers. This may be a good time to pass out the "How to Cite Your Source" information sheet (Figure 4.2). This sheet will go into their I-Search Learning Log for future reference.

GUIDED PRACTICE

Have students work with a partner to find additional information from a different source for the same question.

- Pass out the second article and explain how you found the article.
- Explain to students that they are to work with their partner to find out more information from a second source. Review the above methods for extracting information.
- Have students work together to fill in the note section of their Note Sheet.
- Monitor students and then review answers after they have had ample time to complete the task.
- Next, have students use the "How to Cite Your Source" page to record this source. You may need to provide them with titles, copyright dates, and authors if they are not present on the article.
- Review the appropriate way to cite the source.
- Have students number the first box with the number "1." This stands for source number "1." Have them number the second source with the number "2." If students use these sources again with other questions, then they will only record the appropriate number in the new source box. This will eliminate any redundant work.
- Explain to students that listing the sources on their Note Sheets will help them with their final product. They will be able to list where they found their information by simply referring back to their Note Sheets instead of trying to remember which books and magazines they used.

INPUT, MODELING, AND GUIDED PRACTICE—SECOND PART OF LESSON

Tell students that the summary part of the Note Sheet enables the researcher to put the information in their own words. Model for students how to take the researched information and summarize it. Do the first sentence for the students. Next, call on students to help you formulate the rest of the summary box. Encourage students to add written comments and reactions concerning their notes (see Figure 4.3).

CLOSURE

Pose the following task: Think about how to take notes using the "trash-n-treasure" method. Give students a minute or two to think. Have students turn to their partners to describe the "trash-n-treasure" method to one another. Monitor the students. Ask a couple of students to share with the class. Record responses on chart paper. Hang the chart paper in the room for future reference. Have students place the practice Note Sheet and "How to Cite Your Source" in their I-Search Learning Log.

This activity is adapted with permission from Barbara Jansen's Trash-N-Treasure Notetaking Technique found in the School Library Media Activities Monthly (*Vol. XII, Number 6/February 1996*).

Students will need numerous opportunities to practice the skills of notetaking and citing sources. With beginning researchers, we usually begin the year with class research projects where we take notes together. The above lesson is used with a current topic of study. The more students are given the opportunity to locate and extract information, the better and more successful they will be.

Take the opportunity to monitor students' accomplishments, abilities, and areas of improvement. For example, while monitoring students, teachers may find that students need additional modeling and work looking for the copyright date, author, and article title when citing sources.

Integrating many of these skills into everyday practice will help the task become easier. For example, always read the title and author of anything read aloud to students. Even discuss the copyright date of all learning materials and books. Students will be more successful if they have been exposed to these issues in an integrated manner.

Lastly, there are many different ways in which to use the Note Sheet. It can be modified and adapted to meet the needs of the students. In the past, we have copied the Note Sheets only on white paper. Students seemed to get lost in the sea of white because six to nine Note Sheets were needed per student. One way we have made the Note

Figure 4.3

Note Sheet

Name _Laura Lockhart_   **Topic** _Lake Tahoe_

Question: Where is Lake Tahoe Located?   Discovered, found

Notes	Source
Toigabe National Forest 6,229 ft. above sea level 193 square miles p.	① Scott, Al. (1997). "Lake Tahoe", Compton's Interactive Encyclopedia", (CD-ROM).
Notes Nevada/California Border Northern Sierra Nevada 20 by 10 mile resort center p. 45	② Smith, Bill. Resort USA. Oasis Pub. 1998, P.45.

Summary

Lake Tahoe is a 20 by 10 mile resort center found on the Nevada and California border. It is located in Northern Sierra Nevada in the Toigabe National Forest which is 6,229 feet above sea level.

Sheet easier to use is to make copies on different colored paper. Students are able to use a different color for each one of their research questions. It helps them to organize their work more efficiently. If students need more than just two sources to answer their question, they can get another Note Sheet that is the corresponding color and add additional sources and information. When students are working with the different colors, they use their notes more efficiently and effectively.

Note Sheets are not the only method of taking notes. Students can use notebook paper, note cards, or charts. We have found that the Note Sheet helps the beginning researcher understand the connection between taking notes, citing sources, and summarizing the information. It is an effective method to use before introducing note cards. The Note Sheet should be adapted and/or revised to meet the level and needs of the students.

5 THE SEARCH

"My search was fun, interesting, and a challenge."
Riley Dodge, 4th grade, 1999

Chapters 1 through 4 prepare students for the actual research. This preliminary work ensures success. Students need to go to the library with adequate skills and motivation. Preliminary work with the I-Search prepares them for the important business of research and helps ready them for the challenge. Collaboration with the school librarian is an important component of this part of the I-Search. Online resources in schools are becoming more and more common. The librarian can provide essential instruction in use of these resources. Eleanor Howe affirmed the importance of students using these resources when she wrote, "students should become competent in developing, evaluating, and modifying a variety of electronic search strategies to retrieve needed information from all types of resources" (1998: 33). Experiences such as these serve a dual purpose because:

> students who use electronic access tools practice a variety of thinking skills that span Bloom's taxonomy. Knowledge and comprehension of the variety of traditional and electronic resources form the foundation of information literacy and are used in selecting appropriate materials for an information need. Analysis is used to define a topic and generate related, broader, and narrower search terms. Logical thinking skills are used to select appropriate search strategies and to develop and modify search statements using subject headings and Boolean operators. Information skills are in resource based learning across the curriculum. Students learn to identify and assess citations in order to evaluate the results of their searches and select resources for their use. Evaluating resources and information becomes even more important when the number of available resources increases and especially when using the Internet. In preparing a written or oral report, students synthesize the information they retrieved in a meaningful way as related to their topic or hypothesis (1998: 33).

These powerful learning opportunities prepare students for, "The

Search," the third part of the I-Search paper. The Search is the story of what students have done to find the answers to their questions. It is important to keep a daily journal about what is being accomplished during the actual research. At the end of each session in the library, students use "The Search Log" to briefly describe what they accomplish (see Figure 5.1). In addition, The Search Log is a metacognitive tool that allows students to reflect, evaluate, and plan their search on a daily basis. Students record their thinking and research for use later in the I-Search paper and project.

THE SEARCH LOG

The first line of the log represents the student's reflection of the day's activities; students record what was accomplished. The second line represents the self-evaluation of what was done. The third line gives students a chance to focus and plan the next day's activities. The following is a possible lesson that will help students learn how to use The Search Log.

Figure 5.1

The Search Log

Date _____

What have I accomplished so far? _____

_____

_____

How have I done so far? _____

_____

What do I need to do next? _____

_____

_____

Date _____

What have I accomplished so far? _____

_____

_____

How have I done so far? _____

_____

What do I need to do next? _____

_____

_____

Date _____

What have I accomplished so far? _____

_____

_____

How have I done so far? _____

_____

What do I need to do next? _____

_____

_____

Date _____

What have I accomplished so far? _____

_____

_____

How have I done so far? _____

_____

What do I need to do next? _____

_____

_____

LESSON: THE SEARCH LOG

MATERIALS AND ADVANCE PREPARATION

- Note Sheets with their questions, plus any blank copies students may need
- At least two copies of The Search Log per student (enlarge the page to give younger students more writing room)
- Pencil
- Transparency of The Search Log
- Transparency pens
- Overhead projector
- I-Search Learning Logs

OBJECTIVE

Students will learn to record, plan, and evaluate their research daily.

INTRODUCTION

Explain to students that they will begin researching their topics. Pass out two pages of The Search Log for students to put in their I-Search Learning Log. Explain to students that these forms will serve several purposes for the unit: They will help them review what they have done, evaluate it, and make a plan for additional research, as well as help them when they begin to write The Search part of their paper.

INPUT

Review each line. Students will record what they have done so far in the research on the first line. The second line provides space for students to evaluate their work, and the third line will give them room to make a plan for future research.

MODEL

On the overhead, put a copy of The Search Log. Record what has been done thus far in the I-Search. For example:

- What have I accomplished so far? *On February 20th, I interviewed Mrs. Liza Boone about Lake Tahoe. She has been to the resort many times. I also called the travel agency and had them send travel brochures about the resort.*
- How have I done so far? *I have done pretty good so far. The interview was very informative, and I can not wait to get the pamphlets.*
- What do I need to do next? *I need to go to the school and pub-*

lic libraries to find additional resources. In addition, I need to watch the mail for the travel brochures.

GUIDED PRACTICE

Have students complete the first entry of their logs. Gear the process to the age and level of the students. Model each part one at a time.

PROCESS BREAK

Pose the following question: "How can The Search Log help you with your research and products?"

- Have students think about the answer.
- Next, have them turn to their partners.
- Finally, have them share how they think it will help.

Call on several students for answers to get whole-class feedback and input.

CLOSURE

Explain to students that they will be using this process throughout their research. Encourage them to add to their Search Log whenever they feel it is necessary, not only when the class is filling it out as a whole. For example, if the student happens to conduct an interview, go to the store, or the public library, encourage them to come in the next day, get their Search Log, and record what they did.

LOCATION AND ACCESS OF SOURCES

The first day in the library may be focused primarily on showing students the many resources that are available and helping them decide which will be best. The following is a lesson on location and access of resources. The lesson utilizes a "Pathfinder" to help students locate them (see Figure 5.2). The Pathfinder needs to be customized to the materials and sources available in the library.

Figure 5.2

Pathfinder

Name _____ Topic _____

Use the following sources to locate information about your topic:

1. Online catalog

    Keyword _____

    Title of book _____

    Call number _____

2. Online catalog

    Keyword _____

    Title of book _____

    Call number _____

3. Online catalog

    Keyword _____

    Title of book _____

    Call number _____

4. Encyclopedia

    Title _____

    Volume _____ Page number_____

5. Multimedia encyclopedia

    Keyword _____

    Title of Article _____

6. Reference book

    Volume _____ Page number_____

7. Reference book

    Volume _____ Page number_____

8. Almanac

    Title _____

    Subject _____ Page number_____

Created by Carolyn Willich and Mary Woodard, 1999.

LESSON: LOCATING SOURCES

MATERIALS AND ADVANCE PREPARATION

- A Pathfinder correlated to match the materials of the library
- Transparency of the Pathfinder
- Student copies of the Pathfinder
- Overhead projector and pens
- Dewey Decimal chart
- Transparency of "Brainstorming Keywords" and copies for each student (see Figure 5.3)
- Dictionaries and thesauri
- Computer with access to online databases
- Computer-data projection device or transparencies of screens highlighted
- Schedule library time
- Plan with librarian

OBJECTIVE

Students will use a Pathfinder and brainstorm keywords to locate both print and nonprint resources for their I-Search project in the library media center.

ANTICIPATORY SET

Explain to students that they will begin the school library portion of their research. Compare the search to being a detective. There are many clues in the library that will help them find the answers to their questions. The Pathfinder will serve as their magnifying glass and help them find their answers.

INTRODUCTION

- Review the Dewey Decimal chart to remind students how books are arranged.
  - Call numbers are found on the spine of each book.
  - Call numbers include the Dewey Decimal number and the first letter, or letters, of the author's last name.

INPUT AND MODELING

- Pass out a Pathfinder to each student.

Note: Model the steps that follow.

Figure 5.3

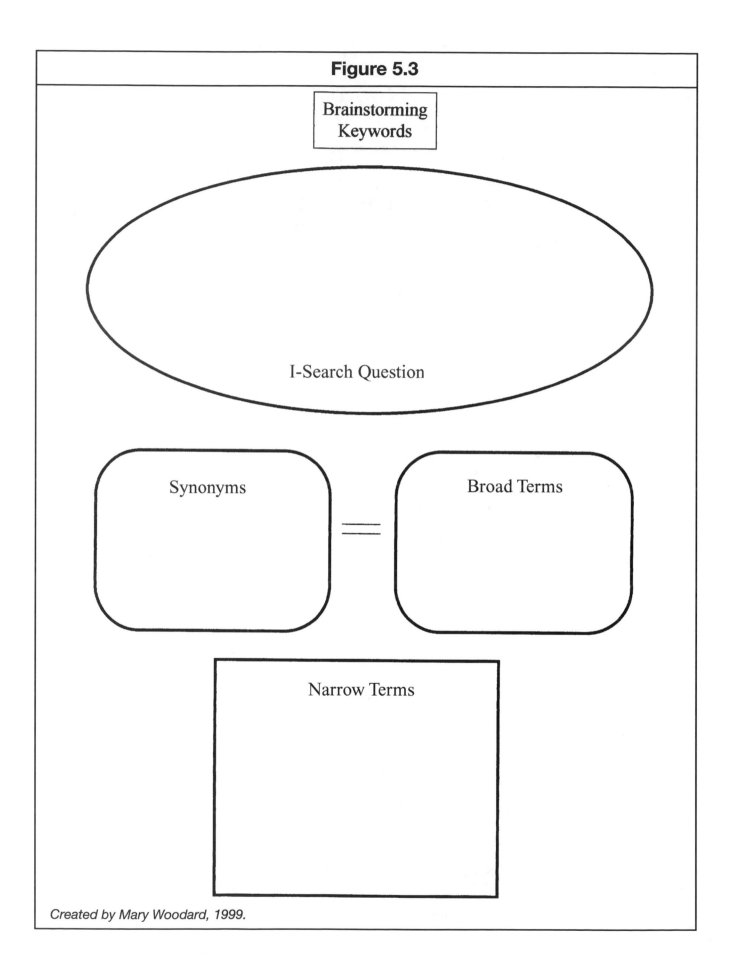

Brainstorming Keywords

I-Search Question

Synonyms

=

Broad Terms

Narrow Terms

Created by Mary Woodard, 1999.

- Fill in the name and topic.
- Demonstrate how to use the online catalog to find a book on their I-Search topic. Begin by defining "online database." A database is a collection of information that is organized so that it can be easily retrieved. If a database is online, that means it can be accessed by a computer. Examples of online databases are the school library online catalog, periodical databases, and reference books. Databases consist of records. The information contained in each record is found in a "field." Use examples from the online catalog to illustrate this concept.
- Go through each step of the process with the students.
  - What sources can I use? Which one is best? Discuss with students the different information that is found in books and periodical articles. Books are good places to find general information on lots of subjects. If the information needed is current, a magazine or newspaper article may be better. Use the example of a horse to illustrate this: If my question is "What are the most important horse races?" a book would probably be the best source. If my question is "Which horse won the Kentucky Derby this year?" the answer would be found in a periodical database. Tell students that today's lesson will concentrate on locating books.
  - Put a transparency of "Brainstorming Keywords" on the overhead. Review keywords. Fill out the transparency using the horse example. Write the question, "What do horses eat?" in the I-Search question box. Look for keywords in the question: *horses* and *eat*. List synonyms for these two words in the synonyms box. Examples of synonyms for *horses* are *livestock* or *equine*. Examples of synonyms for *eat* are *consume*, *dine*, *nibble*, and *devour*. Suggest using a dictionary or thesaurus to help develop a list of synonyms.
  - Together with the students, think of "Broader Terms" for these two keywords (*animals*, *farm animals*, *nutrition*, or *food*).
  - Then think of more "Narrow Terms" such as *stallion*, *Arabian*, or *Persian*.
  - Demonstrate how to access the library online catalog. Do several searches using the words that were brainstormed. Record the titles and call numbers on The Pathfinder.
  - Model for students how to locate a book in the library media center.
  - Evaluate the results of the search. Ask "Did I find a book that will answer my question?"

Note: The above steps to searching is an introduction to the process. As students become more sophisticated with this skill, they can record their keywords on their Note Sheet.

GUIDED PRACTICE

The following activity is based on the availability of online catalog stations. The following is a suggestion:

- Each student or small group of students should be at a computer with access to the online catalog. Have students do a search on their topic by brainstorming keywords and recording their source on The Pathfinder. Help students work through each step.

INDEPENDENT PRACTICE

Have students continue filling out The Pathfinder on their own. Students need to find sources in as many different formats as possible. As students begin to complete their Pathfinder, they may begin collecting their materials.

CLOSURE

- Have students fill out the next section of The Search Log.
- Ask students to identify any problems they may have had, call on students, and record their answers.
- Ask students to identify possible solutions to the problems. These issues may also be good subject matter for the next day's mini-lesson.
- Conclude by having students share their successes.
- Students store The Search Log, The Pathfinder, and the keyword organizer in their I-Search Learning Log.

Note: Students will be able to pull out their Pathfinders the next day and begin their research where they left off the day before. It saves time and energy and helps students use the library more effectively.

The Locating Sources lesson is adapted and reprinted with the permission of Carolyn Willich, librarian at Thompson Elementary in Mesquite ISD, Texas, and Mary Woodard, Library Systems Manager, Mesquite ISD, 1999.

Each day, make notes of the needs and abilities of the students. The mini-lessons will come from these observations. Possible areas for review may include: use of table of contents and index, map of the library, the Dewey Decimal system, online catalogs, use of an encyclopedia index, finding appropriate periodicals, using the online encyclopedia, and locating information on the Internet. The Web is the most powerful of these sources; it has a wealth of information for students to access and use. Unfortunately, as Alan November writes, "the Internet is a place where you can find 'proof' of essentially any belief system that you can imagine and for too many students, 'if it's on the Internet, then it is true'" (1999). November, in his article "The Web—Teaching Zac to Think," tells a true story about a 14-year-old student who comes to the conclusion, as a result of using information he got on the Internet, that the Holocaust never happened. November discusses how students can use the Web itself to evaluate their sources by determining the purpose, author, and Meta Web information of the site found (1999). Teaching students how to use the Internet is crucial to successful searches. Teachers and librarians need to work together to teach lessons on its uses. They may use bookmarks and predetermined search engines to help students access good sites for their searches.

Allow time for students to research. Take the resources to the classroom if time runs out and scheduling additional library time is not an option. Another possibility is to send groups of students to the library during flexible times. Students that finish their research may begin on the summary boxes of their Note Sheets.

Students need to be reminded of their Research Planner and the deadlines. They do not need to be rushed, but rather have a structured setting in which they feel the freedom to explore, discover, and build community. The following is an excerpt of a fifth grader's experience when searching for the answers to her questions. Her name is Cynthia Gayton and her topic was "Why do Kids Take Drugs?"(1995).

First I started my hunt by sharing my question with the class. That helped me get started. They told me places I could go and who to interview. Then I went to the school library on Monday and got a dictionary. That didn't help me at all. J.R. was looking through books and found a book on Marcia's and my topic. That book helped me a lot. The book was called *Health and Drugs*. I thanked J.R. a lot of times for giving me that book. Then on Tuesday I went on looking for a different book. Marcia found one. It was called *Drug Abuse*. Marcia said she would let me use the book. I thanked her. That book helped me get more note cards done. Then I interviewed some kids on Thursday. I asked Chris F., Marcia M., and Kristen T., three questions. I thanked all of them for helping me. Then I went on and interviewed a grown-up on Friday. I interviewed her by phone. I really wanted to interview a cop, but I couldn't. All the cops were really busy. So instead of interviewing a cop I interviewed someone else, my sister. She used to have a friend on drugs. She was a kid. These interviews helped me a lot. I think I have my answer.

Jeremy Holmsley, a third grader, writes of his search experiences on trains (1996):

The search is on. At first I had no luck. But Mrs. Lockhart took us to the school library. I looked in the card catalog. I found six books about trains. I was excited! I read them and only one of them gave one of my answers. So, I said I was going to do an interview with Mr. Prince. He gave me the answers to all of my questions. He also gave me some stuff to show to the class and one of his rewards (awards).

SECTION IV:

HOW WILL I SHOW WHAT I LEARNED?

6 WRITING THE I-SEARCH PAPER

"These are exciting times in the teaching of writing" (Calkins and Harwayne, 1987: 1). Authors such as Nancy Atwell, Lucy Calkins, Donald Graves, and Shelley Harwayne have led the movement to teach children to be better writers. They have authored many wonderful books regarding the writing process and implementation in the classroom. We have attempted to integrate what has been learned from these authors in our approach to teaching the I-Search paper.

"Encouraging students to write about topics that matter most to them is probably the first step in helping students care about their writing" (Calkins and Harwayne, 1987: 23). When students choose their own I-Search topic they are a step closer to caring about their writing and how they will communicate their feelings and findings in informative text.

Students write their I-Search papers using a specific writing-process format. This process includes writing the first draft, revising and editing the draft, peer conferencing, editing and revising, and final copy. Throughout the year, students will probably become very familiar with this process. If students have not been exposed to the writing process, the I-Search unit is one avenue in which to introduce them to the format.

Whether they know it or not, students have been exposed to this writing process throughout the I-Search process. The "Why I Chose This Topic" (Chapter 1) and "What I Knew Before I Started My I-Search" (Chapter 2) sections of the paper have already been written as rough drafts. The rest of this chapter will show possible ways to continue to facilitate the writing process and pull the I-Search paper together.

There are many ways to write the I-Search paper. Each teacher needs to base their writing sessions on the age, level, and experience of the learners in their classroom. For more advanced learners, teachers can work with the paper as a whole (all four sections of the paper being worked on together). For younger, less-experienced learners, teachers may decide to break up the paper by its four sections and work with each component one at a time. For example, students can apply the writing process to the first section, "Why I Chose This Topic." Then they move on and apply the process to "What I Knew Before I Started My I-Search." This continues until all the sections of the paper have been completed. Breaking up the paper by its sections allows the learner to pay close attention to each part and learn the writing process while keeping the paper as a whole in mind. Teachers need to observe the needs of their students in order to determine the best approach.

WRITING THE I-SEARCH PAPER

The suggested lessons in this chapter breaks up the I-Search paper into manageable parts based on the writing process. The lessons are structured as an introduction so they can be adapted to the needs of students. We have also continued to apply the modeling and sharing technique used in previous lessons to enhance the unit and classroom community. As Lucy Calkins writes, "When we share our writing, we uncover and share who we are. Writing invites us to put ourselves on the line, to bring ourselves into the classrooms, into the teaching-learning transaction. And that has made a world of difference" (Calkins and Harwayne; 1987: 21).

WRITING EVALUATION AND ASSESSMENT

To prepare students for the expectations of the writing assignment, have them help develop a rubric for the paper (see Chapter 8). It is a good idea to develop the rubric before students begin writing their paper. The rubric will help them understand the expectations and criteria of the assignment.

LESSON: WHY I CHOSE THIS TOPIC (DAY ONE)

MATERIALS AND ADVANCE PREPARATION
- *On the Bus With Joanna Cole*
- Teacher's transparency on "Why I Chose This Topic"
- Overhead projector
- I-Search Learning Logs
- Student dictionaries
- Chart paper and markers
- Writing Process list (see Figure 6.1)
- List of editing and revision marks (see Figure 6.2)

OBJECTIVE
Students will learn how to apply the skills used by authors and their own learning to write the first section of the I-Search paper, "Why I Chose This Topic." They will also learn about the writing skills of editing and revising.

ANTICIPATORY SET
- Read pages 52 and 53 of Joanna Cole's autobiography. She describes what it is like to be inside the writing. She states that she can be in the middle of writing when suddenly everything begins to move faster and she becomes lost in the process. She describes how she enjoys the writing and cannot wait to get back to the process. She concludes the section by stating, "For me, this is an ordinary part of being a writer, and every time it happens, it's extraordinary" (Cole, 1996: 53).
- Discuss with students how Cole views writing by what she has written in her autobiography.

CONNECTION AND FOCUS
Have students help generate a list of thoughts describing the importance of writing. Have them share their thoughts as well as Joanna Cole's ideas.

INPUT AND MODELING
- Review the writing process format used in class and place the first draft copy of "Why I Chose This Topic" on the overhead.
- Tell students that since they have already written the first draft they will move to the next step of the writing process: revising.
- Read the paper out loud and all the way through.

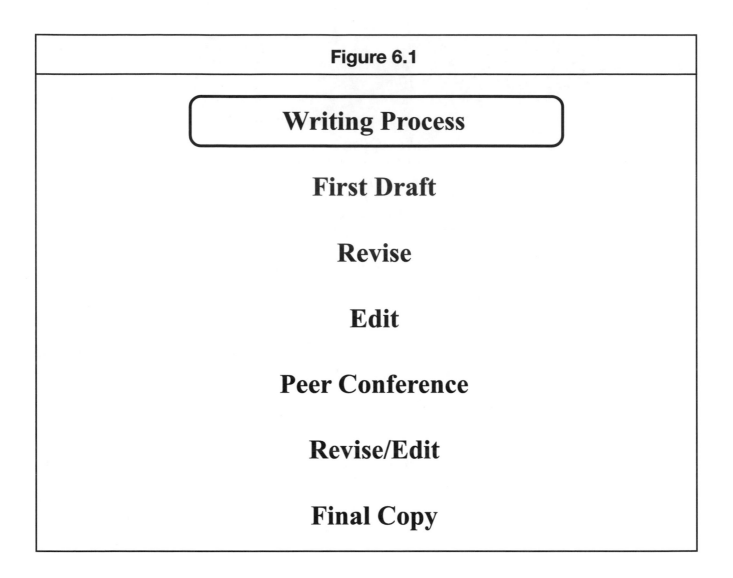

Figure 6.1

Writing Process

First Draft

Revise

Edit

Peer Conference

Revise/Edit

Final Copy

Figure 6.2

Editing and Revising

(-) Put one line through things you want to take out

(^) Use a caret to add letter, words, and/or sentences

 Circle words that are misspelled

(≡) Put three lines under letters that need to be capitalized.

?! Add any end punctuation that is missing

(/) Put a slash through any letters that need to be lowercase

- Ask: "Does it say everything I would like it to say and will it make sense to someone else reading this paper?"
- Discuss with students the following revision marks: caret (^)for adding and a line (–) for taking away.
- Add or take away anything that will help improve the paper. Use the think-aloud process and model revising on the overhead.

GUIDED PRACTICE

- Have students get their "Why I Chose This Topic" from their I-Search Learning Logs.
- Have students read their writing and decide on one thing that they will revise.
- Have them turn to their partners to share what they will revise and how it will help the reader better understand the writing.
- Have them ask their partners if the revision helps them better understand the paper.
- Monitor students to check for understanding.

INDEPENDENT PRACTICE

Have students continue revising their papers. Remind them to reread the writing to make sure that others can understand it.

Note: Move on to the editing portion of the writing process if time allows. Close this lesson and move on to editing the next day if time is short.

CLOSURE AND CHECK FOR UNDERSTANDING

Discuss with students what was learned and how revising improved their writing.

LESSON: WHY I CHOSE THIS TOPIC (DAY TWO)

FOCUS

Review the writing process and what was accomplished the day before.

INPUT AND MODELING

- Review the following editing marks with the students: spelling, paragraphing, capitalization, and punctuation (add anything else that may have been taught during the course of the year)
- The editing marks may be posted for the class to use and see (see Figure 6.2 for list of possible editing and revision marks). Model editing the paper on the overhead. (During the modeling, show how to look up a misspelled word in the dictionary.)

GUIDED PRACTICE

- Have students use the editing chart and choose two things they can edit in their writing of "Why I Chose This Topic."
- Have them edit those two things and then share what they edited with a partner.
- Monitor students to check for understanding.

INDEPENDENT PRACTICE

Have students continue editing their papers using the editing marks and dictionaries. Teacher monitors and conferences with students.

CLOSURE AND CHECK FOR UNDERSTANDING

Discuss what was learned and how it will improve the writing.

Note: With lots of practice, editing and revising becomes a more natural part of the writing process. The more students are able to revise and edit their writing, the more creative and confident they will become. The above lessons are scripted in order to teach the process to beginners.

PEER CONFERENCING

"Conferencing is a face-to-face interaction that yields a reflection of the project at hand" (Fogarty, 1994: 158). Conferencing in the writing-process classroom takes on at least two forms: talking to a peer about the writing and talking with the teacher. "Conferencing is a natural monitoring strategy . . . the classroom that mirrors a philosophy of self-regulatory, developmental learning, also uses conferencing to periodically check on the state of things" (Fogarty, 1994: 158). We have learned that this part of the writing process is very important; however, the organization and structure of conferencing will dictate its success.

The Reading-Writing Workshop: Getting Started, written by Norma Jackson and Paula Pillow, is a wonderful resource for elementary teachers who want to implement a reading and writing workshop in their classrooms. In their book, Jackson and Pillow write about peer conferencing and techniques for teaching students the procedures. The following is a modified version of their lesson about introducing peer conferencing to students:

LESSON: PEER CONFERENCING

MATERIALS AND ADVANCED PREPARATIONS
- "Why I Chose This Topic" paper
- Peer Conferencing Booklet for each student (see Figure 6.3).
- Each student will need at least four pages of the Peer Conference Record (Figure 6.4)
- Prepare a chart that lists the peer conference rules (see Figure 6.5)
- Transparency of Peer Conference Record
- Transparency of teacher's edited and revised "Why I Chose This Topic"

Note: You may want to make the booklets ahead of time for younger learners. Brads or staples are possibilities for putting the booklet together.

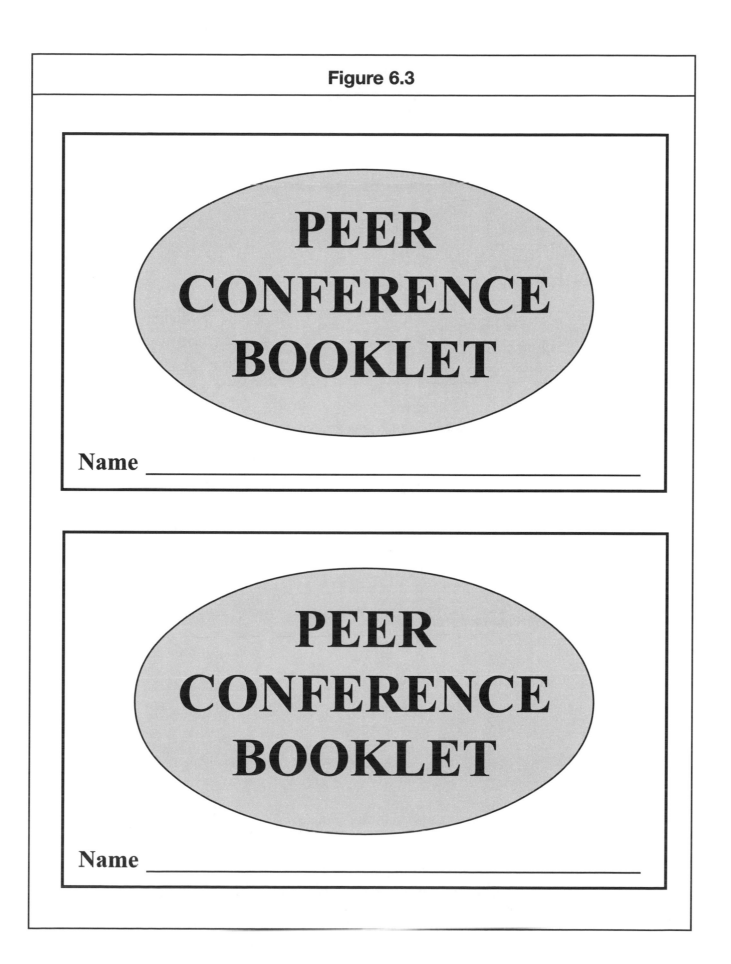

Figure 6.3

PEER CONFERENCE BOOKLET

Name _____

PEER CONFERENCE BOOKLET

Name _____

Figure 6.4

Peer Conference Record

Name _____ Date _____

Title of Writing _____

Conference Partners _____

_____ 1. Read your writing to your partner.

Ask the following questions:

_____ 2. What is my writing about?

_____ 3. What do you like best about my writing?

_____ 4. Did I say anything confusing? _____ What? _____

_____ 5. Do I need to add more details? _____ Where?

_____beginning _____ middle _____ end

_____ 6. Could you read over my paper and help with any spelling, capitalization, and/or punctuation problems?

Summarize what you changed or will change in your writing.

_____

_____

- -

Peer Conference Record

Name _____ Date _____

Title of Writing _____

Conference Partners _____

_____ 1. Read your writing to your partner.

Ask the following questions:

_____ 2. What is my writing about?

_____ 3. What do you like best about my writing?

_____ 4. Did I say anything confusing? _____ What? _____

_____ 5. Do I need to add more details? _____ Where?

_____beginning _____ middle _____ end

_____ 6. Could you read over my paper and help with any spelling, capitalization, and/or punctuation problems?

Summarize what you changed or will change in your writing.

_____

_____

Adapted from The Reading Writing Workshop: Getting Started *by Norma R. Jackson and Paula L. Pillow.* © 1992 *by Scholastic Inc. Reprinted by permission of Scholastic Inc.*

Figure 6.5

Peer Conference Rules

1. **Choose one person to meet with you.**

2. **Confer quietly in a designated conferencing spot.**

3. **Listen respectfully to all writing and ideas.**

4. **The owner of the writing is the only one who writes on the paper.**

5. **Thank your partner for their help.**

6. **Always summarize what you changed and plan to change in your writing.**

Adapted from The Reading Writing Workshop: Getting Started *by Norma R. Jackson and Paula L. Pillow.* © 1992 by Scholastic Inc. Reprinted by permission of Scholastic Inc.

OBJECTIVE

Students will learn peer conference techniques that will help improve their writing.

ANTICIPATORY SET

Direct students to Joanna Cole's collaboration with editors and scientists when she writes and researches.

FOCUS

Explain to students that the purpose of writing is to communicate ideas to others. Writers already understand what they are trying to say, so it is often difficult for them to see where their writing is unclear or needs more details. As a result, writers confer with other people to make their writing better. The author conferences with people with whom they feel comfortable and who will give them honest feedback to make their writing better (Jackson and Pillow, 1992).

CONNECTION

Students will be using the peer conferencing techniques to revise and edit the first portion of their I-Search papers, "Why I Chose This Topic."

INPUT

Discuss the peer conference rules. Pass out the Peer Conference Booklets and discuss how and when to complete each part.

- Record the name, date, title of writing, and partner before beginning the conference.
- Decide who will go first if both parties need a conference.
- The owner of the paper that will be discussed reads their writing to their peer first.
- They then ask the questions one through six and fill out their sheet.
- The owner of the writing is the only person who will be marking on the paper. As a result, both students need to be looking over the writing together while the owner makes corrections and notes.
- Students go back to their desks and fill out what they will change or changed in their writing on the summary section. Students then begin revising and editing their paper one last time.

MODELING

Model a peer conference with one of your students. Choose a student who will give you honest and constructive feedback on your "Why I Chose This Topic" paragraph. Demonstrate the conference rules and use the peer conference record and "Why I Chose this Topic" transparency to move step by step through the conference.

GUIDED PRACTICE

Put students in pairs. Guide students as a class step by step through the peer conference.

- Let students decide who will go first.
- Instruct the students who will be going first to read their writing to their partner.
- Have students ask question two of their partners after the reading.
- Have students ask question three and their partners answer.
- Repeat above process for questions four through six. Teacher monitors students' work and makes notes of positive interactions and areas for improvement.

- Explain to students that they will need to change something in their writing and describe it in the summary section.
- Repeat the above process for the second partner.
- Monitor students and note observations (include positive things as well as areas for improvement).
- Have students fill out their summary sections. Give them a few minutes to make any needed revisions in their writing.

INDEPENDENT PRACTICE

Students will use these techniques on their own in later writing sessions.

CLOSURE

Take the list that you generated while monitoring the groups and share your observations with the class. Praise specific student behavior and reinforce desired behavior. Discuss appropriate ways to handle problem situations.

> **Note: When students are ready to be more become self-directed with their conferences, have pairs of students model the appropriate ways to follow the steps of peer conferencing:**
> - **How to choose a partner in a room of quiet writers**
> - **How to say no if someone asks you for a peer conference and you are busy**
> - **How to quietly gather your materials and go to the appropriate peer conferences area**
> - **How to thank your partners appropriately**
> - **How to get back to work after conducting a peer conference**

From The Reading Writing Workshop: Getting Started *by Norma R. Jackson and Paula L. Pillow.*

Students may begin their final copies of the "Why I Chose This Topic" now, or wait until the entire paper has been through the steps of the writing process. More on the final copy will be explained at the end of this chapter.

WRITING PROCESS FOR THE REMAINDER OF THE PAPER

There are two different methods of continuing to work with students and their writing. One suggestion is to take the rough draft of the section of the I-Search paper "What I Knew Before I Started" and repeat the above process. This would most likely be beneficial for inexperienced and young learners. Another method may be to get the first drafts for "The Search" and "What I Learned" ready and let students then move through the writing process at a self-directed pace. Using this method, the teacher can monitor students through individual conferences and status checklists. Regardless of which method is chosen, the goal is to assess once again the needs and abilities of the students and differentiate the instruction as needed.

COMPONENTS OF THE SELF-DIRECTED WRITING SESSIONS

Good writing sessions might include the following components that are adapted from Lucy McCormick and Shelley Harwayne's *The Writing Workshop: A World of Difference* (1987):

- A teacher-directed meeting, sometimes called a mini-lesson. This gives teachers the opportunity to meet with the class as a whole to discuss specific issues, techniques, and crafts to help make writing better. Student, teacher, and literature examples are often used as models of good writing.
- An in-class writing session. This type of session is used for silent writing through the writing process and peer and teacher conferencing.
- A share session. This closes the writing session. Writers share work in progress to receive additional help from peers.
- Alternative forms of share sessions include students sharing their writing in pairs, in groups, or with parent volunteers.
- Teachers can also use this time to reiterate what was learned in the mini-lessons and how students may have used the information. Teachers may also comment on observations made during the writing sessions.

LESSON: WRITING THE SEARCH

MATERIALS NEEDED AND ADVANCE PREPARATION
- Students' I-Search Learning Log
- The Search Log
- Overhead projector
- Teacher's copy of The Search Log as a transparency
- Student examples of "The Search"

OBJECTIVE
Students will be learning to elaborate lists of facts, dates, feelings, and findings into an interesting story of their I-Search journey.

ANTICIPATORY SET
Reread several examples of students' "The Search." See Appendix and Chapter 5 for such examples.

FOCUS
Ask students how this part of the paper sounds? Is it just a list of people, places, and sources? Or do the students make this section into a story? Discuss the findings and feelings that are expressed in each example.

CONNECTION
Students will use their Search Logs to write "The Search" section of their I-Search paper.

INPUT AND MODELING
- Show the model Search Log on the overhead.
- Place stars by the dates and first line of each entry. These lines will show the heart of their search.
- Read aloud everything that was done to find the answers to research questions. On a separate sheet of paper (blank transparency) begin writing the first draft of "The Search." Be sure to include dates, people, places, and findings in story form.

GUIDED PRACTICE
- Have students review their Search Logs.
- Have them put stars by the dates and first lines to help them focus on the facts.
- Review the ways that other students have started their papers.
- Have students decide on the best topic sentence for this section.

- Have students share their topic sentences with their partners. Call on several students to share their topic sentences. Check for understanding.

INDEPENDENT PRACTICE

Have students use the remainder of the time to work on the rest of "The Search" section of their paper. The teacher monitors and conferences with students.

CLOSURE

Discuss observations made during the writing session. Explain to students that this is their first draft of "The Search" and that they will be taking it through the rest of the writing process.

WHAT I LEARNED

The "What I Learned" section of the I-Search contains the answers to all the research questions and any other interesting information that was discovered. It is not simply a list of answers, but information put together in the author's own words to make an interesting and informative piece of writing. It matches the rest of the paper in its first-person narrative form.

The information and writing from this section will come from the summary boxes of the Note Sheets. There are several ways to approach this section of the paper. One way is to use the summary sections of the Note Sheets as part of the first draft. For example, write editing, revising, and peer conferencing comments directly on the summary boxes of each Note Sheet. Another way to work with the information is to have students use the summary boxes to write their first draft and then have them work through the rest of the writing process. The following lesson shows how to take the summary boxes and create a first draft.

LESSON: WRITING THE FIRST DRAFT OF WHAT I LEARNED

MATERIALS NEEDED
- Student I-Search Learning Logs with all the Note Sheets
- Teacher's or students' examples of Note Sheets on research
- Student examples of "What I Learned"
- Overhead projector
- Blank transparency
- Plain paper for each student

OBJECTIVE
Students will use their Note Sheets to create their first draft of "What I Learned."

ANTICIPATORY SET
Read examples of the "What I Learned" section from student papers. See the appendix for examples. Explain to students that they will be using the summary boxes of their Note Sheets to write their section of "What I Learned."

FOCUS
- Discuss how this part of the paper sounds. Is it a list of facts? Is it straight out of another book? Is the information in the writer's own words? Does the writer express any feelings or emotions?
- Have students think about the answers to the questions and then turn to a partner and discuss them. Call on several students to comment on the writing.

INPUT AND MODELING
- Show students the model Note Sheets on the overhead. Review how the summary boxes were created.

Note: A student's collection of Note Sheets may also be used to model the process with the class.

- Lay all the Note Sheets out so they can be seen all at one time. (This will be difficult to do on the overhead. Taping them to a chalkboard may work better.) Think aloud and decide what information goes together and place these Note Sheets side by side.

- Next, decide what information needs to be first, second, and so forth. Keep in mind what would make sense to the reader.
- Number the Note Sheets according to what order the information needs to appear in the paper.
- Next, begin the first draft by brainstorming an introductory paragraph. Begin writing the information from each Note Sheet in order. (The first couple of Note Sheets may be done so that students get the idea.)
- Finish off by writing the concluding paragraph. Students may change the wording of their summary boxes, but not the facts.

GUIDED PRACTICE

Take students step by step through the above process.

Step 1: Lay out all the Note Sheets.
Step 2: Put Note Sheets with similar subject matter side by side.
Step 3: Begin putting the Note Sheets in the order that makes sense to the reader.
Step 4: Number the Note Sheets.
Step 5: Stack the Note Sheets in the appropriate numerical order.
Step 6: Begin writing the introductory paragraph.

Teacher monitors and conferences with students.

INDEPENDENT PRACTICE

- Students continue writing the first draft of their paper using their ordered Note Sheets until they finish with their concluding paragraph.
- The teacher monitors the writing and designates students to share during the closing part of the session.

CLOSURE

Discuss observations made during the writing session. Have students share what they have accomplished. Discuss the writing using constructive feedback.

FINAL COPIES

There are many different ways to publish the I-Search paper. It may be entered into the computer, typed, handwritten, or made into an I-Search book. Pictures of the students with their projects can also be included in their published material. Only the imagination limits the number of ways students can publish their I-Search papers.

7 DEVELOPING AND PRESENTING THE I-SEARCH PROJECT

In this chapter...
- Choosing an I-Search Project
- Developing a Rubric for the Products
- Designing the Product
- I-Search Project Contracts
- Presenting the I-Search Project and Developing Communication Skills
- Lesson: Introduction and Eye Contact
- Lesson: Speaking Clearly (Diction) and Volume
- Lesson: Posture and Gestures
- Lesson: Organization
- Communication Skills Rubric
- Presentation Days

Helping students to become successful lifelong learners requires utilizing learning activities that are performance based, that initiate active learning, and that are rooted in authentic assessment. Active lifelong learners need "to figure things out by themselves; generate their own examples; trust their own hypotheses; demonstrate their own skills; assess their own competencies; determine the qualities of their efforts; apply what they have learned to new situations; and teach others what they have learned" (Silver, Strong, Commander, 1998: 1). This chapter is devoted to helping teachers continue these types of learning experiences in the I-Search unit by helping students develop and present their projects.

In Chapter 6, we discussed how students can show what they have learned through the I-Search paper. The process of writing and working through the paper is very important to the learning; however, we feel students also need the opportunity to synthesize their learning in other ways.

Choice in products (the way students choose to present their I-Search projects) is a very important component of the I-Search unit. Students are able to look at their research, and decide the best way to show and present their learning. Having students decide on their project during the planning stages of the I-Search is important (see the lesson on Research Planners in Chapter 2). Teachers and students can brainstorm the possibilities of products while completing the Research Planner. This gives students direction for their research: however, students need to have the freedom to change their mind when they see their research taking a new direction. In the middle—or near the end—of their search, they may decide a diorama would show their learning much better than a poster. The following is one way teachers can facilitate the I-Search project choice.

CHOOSING AN I-SEARCH PROJECT

Step One: Have students think about possible ways to demonstrate their learning. You may want to give a partial list to students if they are having difficulty thinking of possible products.

Possible I-Search Projects:

- Diorama
- Poster
- Big book
- Puppet show
- Song/rap
- Graphic organizer
- Model
- Multi-media project
- Mobile
- News cast

Step Two: Have students study the list. They may also think of their topic and the research they will be doing or have done. Ask them to decide which I-Search project will help them to best communicate their findings to an audience.

Step Three: Have students record their project in Step 4 of the I-Search Research Planner. If this was done early in the planning stages, give students the option to change their project if they feel they can demonstrate their learning better in another way. This helps them develop the ability to be in charge of their learning process, product, assessment, and evaluation.

DEVELOPING A RUBRIC FOR THE PRODUCTS

Student- and teacher-developed rubrics are very powerful. They give students ownership over their learning and assessment. As a result, students are more likely to understand and follow the guidelines for a good product.

As a result, students can be grouped by their product choices to develop their rubrics. The forms are the same. This allows students to become increasingly efficient the more they create.

Note: See Chapter 8 for more on developing rubrics and examples of student- and teacher-created rubrics.

DESIGNING THE PRODUCT

Before students begin working on their product, it is extremely important for them to create, know, and understand the criteria for evaluation. Once the rubrics have been developed for each product, make copies for the students to use while they are creating their I-Search projects. This helps students become familiar with the criteria and to check it while working on their projects.

Depending on time and resources, students may work on their I-Search projects at home or at school. Inform parents and guardians of the plan and requirements in either instance. Having students work on their projects at home frees up classroom time and allows parents to provide additional input in the process. Completing the projects in class, however, allows for additional collaboration between the students. They help one another and offer support and supplies while each works on their own individual projects.

If students are doing their I-Search projects at home, make copies of their I-Search papers or their Note Sheets. Also, include a copy of the appropriate rubric. This helps the development of the project to be more effective.

I-SEARCH PROJECT CONTRACTS

The I-Search project contract is another way to let students and parents understands the expectations and responsibilities of having their work completed on time. About a week to ten days before the projects and presentations are due, send the contract home along with a copy of their chosen rubric and research information (see Figure 7.1). The contracts should be returned as soon as possible and kept on file.

PRESENTING THE I-SEARCH PROJECT AND DEVELOPING COMMUNICATION SKILLS

"Building strong communication skills can help us unlock the door to better self understanding" (Marrs, 1992: 1). Demonstrations and performances are also another form of authentic assessment. These "require communication skills which are necessary for success in the workforce of today and the future. Students learn to organize information and present their views and facts in an interesting format for an audience" (Nagel, 1996: 109).

Communication skills and strategies should be introduced as early as possible in the year. Students are then able to build on the skills throughout the year in many different ways. The more experience they have using their skills, the more opportunity they will have to grow, learn, and have confidence being in front of an audience.

A third grader who was participating in an I-Search unit for the first time demonstrated his communication skills growth in a powerful way. Robert was shy and insecure. The communication unit was taught at the beginning of the year. The students then presented their findings for the culminating research project. When it was Robert's turn to present his project, he was extremely nervous, fidgety, and unprepared. At one point during the presentation, he looked at the teacher and shouted "What?" We began thinking that maybe some children are just not mature enough to handle the pressures of oral speaking. At the end of the day, however, he announced that it was fun, and he was not going to be as scared doing his presentations at church.

By the end of the year, and many presentations later, Robert was a pro. His last presentation included a diorama and paper. He had prepared notes to keep him organized and on track. He enunciated his words, made eye contact, and used his visual aids to describe all that he had learned. The practice throughout the year and our classroom

Figure 7.1

I-SEARCH PROJECT

CONTRACT

My project is going to be a _____. My presentation and project will include all the answers to my questions and any additional information I feel is important. I will follow the specific guidelines found on the rubric (attached). I will have my project ready at the beginning of class on

_____.

Student_____

Parent _____

Teacher _____

Please return this sheet. You may keep the attached rubric at home in order to check the requirements while working on your project. Thank you and have fun!

environment had allowed Robert to become a confident and effective presenter. He learned good speaking skills that will serve him well in the future. He also developed self-confidence and had a new sense of pride about his ability to speak before a group.

The following are suggested lessons to teach communication skills. They will need to be modified and extended depending on the level of the students.

LESSON: INTRODUCTION AND EYE CONTACT

MATERIALS NEEDED AND ADVANCE PREPARATION
- Video of newscaster or another person giving a speech
- VCR
- Stars for each student
- Poster showing points to remember
- Familiar story or poem for students to read
- Student I-Search Learning Logs

OBJECTIVE
Students will be introduced to the communication unit and learn to apply the skill of eye contact.

ANTICIPATORY SET
Show a five-minute clip of the video. Discuss good and bad communicators. What skills make a good speaker? What skills make a bad speaker? (Brainstorm with the class on the overhead or board.)

INTRODUCTION
Explain to students that they will be learning the skills to help them become effective speakers. The first skill that will be discussed is eye contact.

BACKGROUND
Explain to students that eye contact is very important to being a good speaker. There are many benefits to having good eye contact. These include:

- Eye contact shows that you are truly interested in the listeners. Look at each person for two to three seconds.
- Looking at someone shows them you are open and honest.

- Eye contact involves the audience and helps keep them interested in what you are saying.

(Vassallo, 1990: 30)

POINTS TO REMEMBER

Explain to students that there are several points to remember when they are working on the skill of eye contact:

- Eye contact should begin the moment you are introduced.
- Memorize your introduction so you will be free to look at the audience.
- Move your eye contact to different sections of the audience.
- Avoid reading too much to the audience. Summarize the information so you can glance up every few seconds.

(Vassallo, 1990: 30–31)

GUIDED PRACTICE

Explain the following activity to the class. Be sure to model the process first.

- Divide the class in half or fourths.
- Each student gets a star or other visual (a thumbs up can also be used).
- Pass out the story or poem to students. Read it and give students a chance to memorize the first line or so.
- Students then take turns reading or summarizing the passage.
- Each audience member holds a star in their lap. They hold the star up when the speaker has made eye contact with them for three seconds (thumbs up can also be used).
- The goal is to have all the stars up.
- The teacher monitors the group.

Note: Students will be able to do independent practice when they do their presentations at the end of the unit.

CLOSURE AND JOURNAL WRITING

Review with students what was learned. In their I-Search Learning Logs, have students create a communication page. Their first assignment is to record the date and then the definition of eye contact. Have students then draw a picture to the side of the definition that will help them remember the meaning. The teacher monitors. Have a few students share their pictures and explain why it helps them to remember the definition.

LESSON: SPEAKING CLEARLY (DICTION) AND VOLUME

MATERIALS NEEDED AND ADVANCE PREPARATION
- Video clip of newscaster or other presenter
- Points to remember poster
- Poems that use alliteration (for example, Peter Piper)
- Student I-Search Learning Logs

OBJECTIVE
Students will learn and practice the skills of diction, volume, and rate.

ANTICIPATORY SET
Show students the video clip. Discuss how the person sounds. What things do they notice about the person's voice and the way he/she pronounces words?

INTRODUCTION
"What you say is important, but the way you say your words is critical—if you are to be understood" (Vassallo, 1990: 44). Speaking clearly will help your audience understand and appreciate what you are saying. The appropriate volume helps the audience hear you comfortably.

POINTS TO REMEMBER
- Open your mouth when you speak.
- Move your lips.
- Practice putting on the final consonant sounds.
- Slow down, but don't go too slow (rate).

(Vassallo, 1990: 45)

MODELING AND GUIDED PRACTICE
Use a poem that shows alliteration. Model for students how to recite the poem while speaking clearly and using the correct volume.
- Pass out the poems.
- Recite the poem together as a class.
- Have students recite the poem to their partners.
- The teacher monitors.

Note: Give students the opportunity to record their voice and then listen to it. Encourage them to evaluate their volume and diction.

CLOSURE AND JOURNAL WRITING

Discuss what was learned. Have students record speaking clearly, volume, and rate with the definitions in their Learning Log. Also, have students design a picture that represents the three. The teacher monitors and leads a class discussion.

LESSON: POSTURE AND GESTURES

MATERIALS AND ADVANCE PREPARATION
- Have students bring an object from home to share with the class (examples include a tennis racket, pen, gum, newspaper, or telephone)
- Teacher needs to bring an object
- Video clip of newscaster or other presenter (a clip of a weather person will help students see how posture and gestures are important to presentations)
- Student I-Search Learning Logs

OBJECTIVE
Students will define and learn the importance of posture and gestures.

ANTICIPATORY SET
Show students the video clip. Ask students what the presenter is doing with his/her hands and body. Do the movements (or lack of movements) distract or help with understanding what the presenter is trying to say? Why? Have students discuss the answer with their neighbors. Lead a class discussion and record answers on the board or overhead.

INTRODUCTION
Discuss with students the facts that people respond 55 percent to your body language and expression, 37 percent to the way you speak, and only 8 percent to what you say (Vassallo, 1990: 27). This means that the way the body moves and the way the hands are used is very important to a good presentation.

POINTS TO REMEMBER
- Stand straight. Pretend to have a book on your head; however, do not stand stiff.
- Avoid playing with your hands. For example, do not play with jewelry, cross your arms in back or in front, or put your hands in your pocket.

- Use natural sweeping movements with your hands.
- Avoid turning your back to the audience.

MODELING AND GUIDED PRACTICE

Model the following activity for students:

- Have students bring an object to class.
- The object needs to be a practical object.
- Divide the class in half or fourths.
- Show the object and completely describe it.
- Explain the uses of the object. These may be practical, humorous, or both.
- Tell anything else that pertains to the object which may be of interest to the audience.
- The speech may be either informative or entertaining.
- Time limit for the speech is one to two minutes (Marrs, 1992: 22)

Explain to students that they need to remember the points of using good posture and gestures while maintaining eye contact and speaking clearly. Monitor the groups.

CLOSURE AND JOURNAL WRITING

Review what was learned. Have students list gesture and posture in their I-Search Learning Log. Have students define each and draw a picture that represents them. The teacher monitors. Discuss as a class.

LESSON: ORGANIZATION

MATERIALS NEEDED AND ADVANCE PREPARATION

- 5 × 7 note cards for the students (five to six per child)
- I-Search papers
- Transparency of model presentation to organize
- Video
- Overhead with overhead pens
- Poster of points to remember
- Student I-Search Learning Logs

OBJECTIVE

The student will use organizational strategies to organize their I-Search speech.

ANTICIPATORY SET

Refer to or show the video clip again. Talk about how the newscasters and/or presenters are organized. Do they ramble with their information? Is their information sequenced?

INTRODUCTION

- "The organization of a presentation is like the foundation of a house: it makes sense to spend some time on it before putting up the walls" (Leech, 1993: 74).
- Discuss this quote with students.
- The organization of the speech will determine how successful it is. A poorly organized speech will confuse the audience and a properly organized speech will help the audience to understand your message.

POINTS TO REMEMBER

- Design the speech in three parts: introduction, body, and conclusion.
- Open with an "eye catcher"—to get their attention. Examples of eye catchers include: putting on a train conductor's hat and asking "Have you ever played with a toy train and wondered how big trains run? I have always been fascinated with trains"; putting on an apron and saying "I used to make mud pies for hours in the back yard. Because of this desire to create, I have found that I love to cook"; telling jokes; posting a quote; or showing a cartoon dealing with the subject matter discussed in the presentation.
- Write key points on note cards. Note cards allow frequent eye contact with the audience since you are not tied to your paper.
- Memorize your introduction and conclusion.
- Be sure to use your visual aids to help the audience understand your information.

(Leech, 1993)

MODELING AND GUIDED PRACTICE

Model the following activity on the overhead and then walk the students through each step while they work on their own presentation.

- On the first note card, have students record their eye catcher. They need to use treasure words to record their information. The treasure words will help the students when they glance at their note card in order to remember the information.
- Read over "Why I Chose This Topic" portion of the I-Search

paper. Record the treasure words that will help with remembering the information. Memorize the introduction so eye contact and interest can be maintained with the audience.

- The body of the paper will include three major points:
  - The first point is "What I Knew Before I Started My I-Search." Read that section of the I-Search paper and record treasure words on the second note card.
  - The second point is "The Search." Read over "The Search" section and record the treasure words on the third note card.
  - The third point is "What I Learned." Read that section of the paper and record the treasure words on the fourth note card. A fifth note card can also be used if needed. Encourage students to also use their visual aids to show what they learned.

- On the last note card, have students record their conclusion using treasure words. "State in the final moments what you want your audience to take away from the presentation" (Vassallo, 1990: 98). The conclusion needs to be strong. Use it as a review and an opportunity to provide one last punch to the presentation. Examples of conclusions with punch include passing out cookies to the audience at the end of a presentation on cooking; blowing a train whistle to demonstrate what a conductor hears every day when he/she goes to work; sharing a meaningful event or idea from the research; or interesting quotes, facts, and cartoons related to the presentation. Encourage students to memorize their conclusion in order to strengthen their presentation.

When students finish their note cards, have them begin working on memorizing their introduction and conclusion. They may also practice giving their speech with a partner. Encourage students to take their note cards home to practice in front of their family members and the mirror.

CLOSURE AND JOURNAL WRITING

Ask students how organizing their speech will help their presentation. Have them discuss with a partner. Brainstorm as a class. Have students add organization to their list of good communication skills. Have students draw a picture that will help them remember the meaning. The teacher monitors. Have students share their pictures and why it helps them remember the definition. Discuss as a class.

This lesson is reprinted with permission from Lisa Barron, Communication Consultant, Dallas, Texas. 1999.

COMMUNICATION SKILLS RUBRIC

Develop a rubric to use for the I-Search Presentations (see Chapter 8).

PRESENTATION DAYS

These are such exciting days. All the hard work has been culminated into a celebration of the student's accomplishments. If at all possible "expand the scope of the audience by getting the students out of their classroom environment or by bringing an audience into the educational setting. The more the audience is valued by the students, the greater the impact will be" (Rogers and Graham, 1998: 13).

The presentations may be spread over three days or they may be presented all in one day. Post a sign-up sheet so other teachers can plan to come. This will help to avoid too many teachers in the room or having no one show up.

We have discussed the importance of good communication skills quite extensively. It is important to not forget the listening skills required from a good audience. Before the presentations begin, discuss audience etiquette. Students should listen with their whole body. For example, they need to make eye contact and listen to what the speaker is really saying. After the presentation, students will be asked to give positive comments or ask questions. Before the presentations, discuss appropriate comments and questions. Students' listening skills may be assessed by having them take notes after each person presents (see Figure 7.2). This also gives students something to do between presentations as presenters take down and set up their projects.

Celebrate the person on stage. They have spent many weeks on their project and have become experts on their topics. Let them answer questions about their learning and their projects. At the conclusion of the presentations, the projects and papers can be displayed for the whole school to see. Be sure to get pictures of the students with their projects. They can use these pictures as cover sheets to their papers. As a result, others will be able to put a face with each project.

Figure 7.2

PRESENTATIONS

Name _____ Date _____

_____
Presenter   Topic

What I Learned

_____
Presenter   Topic

What I Learned

_____
Presenter   Topic

What I Learned

_____
Presenter   Topic

What I Learned

_____
Presenter   Topic

What I Learned

_____
Presenter   Topic

What I Learned

_____
Presenter   Topic

What I Learned

_____
Presenter   Topic

What I Learned

SECTION V:

HOW WILL I KNOW
I DID A GOOD JOB?

Chapter 8: Teacher and Student

Assessment and Evaluation

8
TEACHER AND STUDENT ASSESSMENT AND EVALUATION

In this chapter...

- Lesson: Developing the I-Search Paper Rubric
- I-Search Project Rubrics
- Communication Rubric
- Student Self Evaluation
- Scoring the Rubrics
- Other Assessments and Evaluations

"During my I-Search I learned how to do research. I will be able to use what I learned again when I do another research project."

Emily Cleveland, 1996

"I feel like I did a good job on my project. I included all the things I found out about rain forest trees."

Courtney Wagner, 1996

"I included all the things I found out about trains. The thing I did best was the interview."

Jeremy Holmsley, 1996

"The thing I liked most about doing this project was researching, because it was a big challenge."

Justin McLearen, 1997

The third graders who made the above comments were active participants in the ongoing assessment and evaluation of their I-Search projects. The participation empowered the students, helped their confidence to grow, and strengthened our community of learners.

Educators use many types of evaluation and assessments. "Typically, evaluation refers to a judgment about student knowledge, student behavior, attitude, or performance. Assessment is a strategy used to gather data (often continuously) about student learning" (Nagel, 1996: 103). The I-Search lends itself to several different types of authentic and ongoing assessment and evaluation. Since many of the assessments are ongoing, they have already been mentioned in previous chapters. For example, "showing what you know through a performance or demonstration allows students to display their knowledge and learning in an active exhibit" (Nagel, 1996: 109).

The I-Search paper and Learning Log provide many opportunities for writing and the writing process. "When classroom time is set aside on a regular basis for reflection, with writing viewed as a tool for thinking and learning, students have the opportunity to create meaning for their work of real-world problem solving within an authentic context" (Nagel, 1996: 110).

Lastly, the Research Planner information problem-solving model allows for an evaluation of the overall process with an end-of-the-unit checklist. This checklist is developed in the beginning and then used for evaluation at the end. The I-Search Learning Log can also serve as an ongoing assessment of student work. The work can be studied and used by both the teacher and student throughout the entire I-Search process.

In each of the above-mentioned forms of authentic assessment, rubrics can be used to provide additional authenticity to the I-Search unit. "A rubric is any established set of statements (criteria) that clearly, precisely, accurately, and thoroughly describe the varying, distinguishable, quality levels that may exist in something or in an action" (Rogers and Graham, 1998: 197).

The I-Search unit uses two types of formal assessment and evaluation. These include Primary Trait rubrics and Performance Checklists. The Primary Trait rubrics focus on a particular trait (Rogers and Graham, 1998). When we focus on the characteristics of a good oral speech or an effective diorama, we are using a Primary Trait rubric. The convenient aspect of this type of rubric is that a general rubric can be developed and then modified to create a series of different primary trait rubrics (Rogers and Graham, 1998). For example, we use the same rubric format for the I-Search paper, presentation, and project. We simply change the traits in each format.

The second type of formal assessment we use in the I-Search unit is the Performance Checklist. "A checklist is precisely what the word implies: a list of items to be checked-off as they are completed or observed during evaluation" (Rogers and Graham, 1998: 206). The checklist when applied in the I-Search unit is found in Step 5 of the Research Planner information problem-solving model. The checklist developed by the teacher and students allows everyone involved to agree upon the "criteria for credit" (Rogers and Graham, 1998).

The rubric and checklist provide an authentic form of assessing students. This assessment can become even more powerful when students have a hand in the development and self assessment of the criteria. Students are empowered when they help to develop the rubrics and, in turn, have the opportunity to evaluate themselves. The learning is more directed and the accountability is more meaningful. When students are involved, learning, evaluation, and assessment are not things that simply happen, they become an integrated and meaningful partnership between the students and teacher.

The following is a suggested lesson on how to develop the I-Search writing rubric with students. The lesson has been adapted from the Rogers, Ludington, and Graham's work on "Standards of Excellence" from their book *Motivation and Learning* (1998).

LESSON: DEVELOPING THE I-SEARCH PAPER RUBRIC

MATERIALS NEEDED AND ADVANCE PREPARATION

- Examples of three exemplary I-Search papers. The three models should have similar characteristics that make them good models, but they should also be somewhat diverse. The models do not have to be perfect, but they should show that the student was displaying skill, ability, and knowledge in the completed writing. Provide enough copies for each group of students.
- An example of an I-Search paper that needs improvement. This can be created by the teacher. Provide enough copies for each group of students.
- Three pieces of chart paper
- Markers in various colors
- Tape
- Blank notebook paper for each group of students

Note: This lesson is intended to be given before students begin writing their I-Search paper. As a result of developing the rubric, students will know and understand the requirements, quality criteria, and expectations of the paper.

OBJECTIVE

Students will be engaged in the development of a rubric for the I-Search paper.

ANTICIPATORY SET AND INTRODUCTION

Tell students that, before they will begin working on their I-Search paper, they will need to know the criteria, requirements, and expectations for the paper. Tell students that today they will help to develop these components.

INPUT, MODELING, AND GROUP WORK

- Divide the class into random groups of two to five depending on their group processing skills.
- Have students decide or assign a writer, two readers, and a material collector.
- Give the groups the three well-written I-Search papers.
- Ask the groups to begin comparing the three model I-Search papers in order to identify the three to five characteristics they have in common. Let them know that you will interrupt the process shortly to provide them with an I-Search paper that needs improvement to help them focus their discussions.
- Have the readers read aloud the papers.
- Teacher monitors the groups.
- When it seems that the "needs improvement" example would be helpful, pass it out to the groups.

GUIDED PRACTICE

- While the groups are working, put three sheets of chart paper on the wall labeled as follows:
  - Characteristics that we all observe.
  - Characteristics that most of us observe.
  - Characteristics that at least one group observes.
- Have Group One report one characteristic of an outstanding paper.
- Poll the other groups.
- Have a recorder place the characteristic on the appropriate piece of chart paper.
- Repeat the above process with each group and/or until all the characteristics have been recorded.
- Have the groups discuss what is on the non-unanimous charts and decide if what is there should be moved to "characteristics we all observe."
- Discuss with students the final agreement. Make sure that everyone agrees and understands the terms.

CLOSURE AND REFLECTION

- Ask students to think about the following question: "How will you be able to use this criteria when writing your I-Search paper?"
- After students think about their comments, have them share with a partner.

- Lead a class discussion on the posed question.

Lesson adapted from "Standards of Excellence" in Motivation and Learning *by Rogers, Ludington, and Graham. © 1997, 1998 Peak Learning Systems, Inc.*

As a result of the above lesson, our students were able to be part of the process of creating the rubric. When this lesson was done with a fourth-grade class, they came up with the following criteria: punctuation, spelling, information, I-Search form, clear and descriptive, bibliography, and deadline. The teacher, or even the students, are then able to take the criteria and plug them into an already existing format. The existing format we use has the levels of quality which include outstanding, good, satisfactory, needs improvement, and not scorable. The teacher and/or the students will then be able to come up with quality statements for each level of the criteria (see Figure 8.1). The leveled statements make it very clear to the students and the teacher what the expectations are for the paper and/or project. As a result, evaluation of the project becomes more objective.

Figure 8.1

Name _____ **Date** _____ I-SEARCH PAPER RUBRIC

	punctuation	spelling	information	I-Search form	clear and descriptive	bibliography	deadline
Outstanding 4	No punctuation errors	No spelling errors	Accurate information—all research questions are answered	All five sections are labeled and complete	Consistently understandable and descriptive	At least three sources completely recorded	Turned in on time or before
Good 3	One to three punctuation errors	One to three spelling errors	Good information—most of the research questions are answered	Most of the sections are labeled and complete	Understandable and descriptive	At least three sources	Turned in by the end of the day on the due date
Satisfactory 2	Several punctuation errors	Several spelling errors	Satisfactory information—half of the questions are answered	Some of the sections are labeled and complete	Some confusion and lacking description	Two sources used	One to two days late
Needs Improvement 1	Paper very difficult to understand due to the amount of punctuation errors	Paper very difficult to understand due to the amount of spelling errors	Incomplete information—less than half of the questions were answered	None of the sections are labeled and the paper is incomplete	Very confusing and no description	One source used for research	Three or more days late
Not Scorable 0	Task not attempted	Task not attempted	Task not attempted	Task not attempted	Task not attempted	Task not attempted	Task not attempted
Student							
Teacher							

I-SEARCH PROJECT RUBRICS

The above process can also be done while developing the I-Search project rubrics. Attempt to find outstanding examples of each I-Search project for these rubrics. The teacher can pull groups of students together to develop the appropriate rubric. For example, those students who have chosen to show their learning with a poster will work together to develop the poster rubric. See Figure 8.2 for an example of a student- and teacher-developed poster rubric.

Figure 8.2

Name _____ Date _____

I-SEARCH POSTER RUBRIC

	punctuation	spelling	information	display	pictures and words	bibliography	deadline
Outstanding 4	No punctuation errors	No spelling errors	Accurate information—all research questions are answered	Poster is very neat and attractive	Words and pictures demonstrate learning and are able to be seen from a distance	At least three sources listed	Turned in on time or before
Good 3	One to three punctuation errors	One to three spelling errors	Good information—most of the research questions are answered	Poster is neat and attractive	Words and pictures demonstrate learning	At least three sources used	Turned in by the end of the day on the due date
Satisfactory 2	Several punctuation errors	Several spelling errors	Satisfactory information—half of the questions are answered	Poster is neat	Words and pictures are included	Two sources used	One to two days late
Needs Improvement 1	Poster very difficult to understand due to the amount of punctuation errors	Poster very difficult to understand due to the amount of spelling errors	Incomplete information—less than half of the questions were answered	Poster is messy and unorganized	Minimal pictures and words are used	One source used	Three or more days late
Not Scorable 0	Task not attempted	Task not attempted	Task not attempted	Task not attempted	Task not attempted	Task not attempted	Task not attempted
Student							
Teacher							

COMMUNICATION RUBRIC

The communication rubric can also be modified from the above lesson. It is important to develop the rubric after the unit has been taught and before presentations are given. For examples of outstanding presentations, the teacher may want to use video recordings of past presentations of merit. The teacher may also refer students to the posters, criteria, and notes from a previously taught communications unit. See Figure 8.3 for an example of a student-and-teacher-developed communication rubric.

Figure 8.3

Name _____ Date _____ COMMUNICATION RUBRIC

	eye contact	posture and gestures	volume and speed	visual aids	speaking clearly (diction)	organization	deadline
Outstanding 4	Presenter makes consistent eye contact with the audience	The presenter uses hands and body in appropriate ways that help the speech	The presenter speaks at a very even speed and is not too loud or too soft	Presenter uses visual aids very effectively. They help with understanding	Presenter speaks very clearly and is easy to understand	Presenter is very organized—note cards and visual aids are used and well planned	Presentation is ready before or the morning of the due date
Good 3	The presenter makes eye contact with the audience most of the time	The presenter uses hands and body in appropriate ways	The presenter speaks at an even speed and the volume is good	Presenter uses visual aids effectively	Presenter speaks clearly	Presenter is organized—note cards and visual aids are used	Presentation is ready at the time of the speech
Satisfactory 2	The presenter makes eye contact with the audience some of the time	The presenter uses hands and body in ways that are distracting some of the time	The presenter speaks at a fair volume and rate	Presenter uses visual aids satisfactorily	Presenter speaks clearly some of the time	Presenter is somewhat organized—has note cards and visual aids	Presentation is ready by the end of the day it is due
Needs Improvement 1	The presenter makes eye contact occasionally	The presenter uses hands and body in ways that are distracting to the speech	The presenter is difficult to understand due to problems in volume and rate	Presenter uses visual aids ineffectively. Speech is not understood	Presenter does not speak clearly and is difficult to understand	Presenter is disorganized. The presentation is hard to follow	Presentation is ready a day or more after the due date
Not Scorable 0	Task not attempted	Task not attempted	Task not attempted	Task not attempted	Task not attempted	Task not attempted	Task not attempted
Student							
Teacher							

STUDENT SELF EVALUATION

In each of the rubrics, students are able to score themselves. Use a rubric that everyone will be using the first time students evaluate themselves. For example, the I-Search Paper Rubric could be used with the whole class to learn the process of scoring. Pass out the rubric for each student. Then have students take out their I-Search papers. Go through the rubric one criteria at a time, reading aloud each quality statement. Have students study their papers for that specific criteria and grade themselves. Repeat the above process for each criteria.

SCORING THE RUBRICS

Grades are a fact of life for most of us. As a result, we may need to be able to derive a grade from these rubrics to place in the grade book. The format of all the rubrics allows the scoring to be flexible. For example, the I-Search Paper Rubric has seven criteria while the Model Rubric has five. As a result of the differing number of criteria, the scoring will differ with each rubric. The teacher and/or students will determine the number required for getting an "A," "B," "C," "D," or "F." For example, in the I-Search Paper Rubric the student and teacher columns are added together and then totaled. An "A" could be between 50 and 56. These numbers are flexible and should be determined in a fair and objective manner.

OTHER ASSESSMENTS AND EVALUATIONS

Many of the evaluations and assessments are ongoing in the I-Search unit. The following is a list of possible things that need to be monitored and potentially evaluated in a formal manner:

- I-Search Learning Log (checked for completion)
- Note Sheets
- Research Planner (checked for completion)
- Research Planner Step 5 checklist (students check off before they turn in their project and paper)
- Writing-process and peer-conference record
- Group work and cooperation

- Self-evaluation written paragraph (see Figure 8.4). This can be added to the I-Search paper, project, and/or unit display. It allows students to assess the process, evaluate what was done well and what could have been done better, and make plans for the future.

Authentic assessment and evaluation are embedded in the I-Search unit. Students and teachers work together to constantly monitor the process, progress, and accomplishments. The cooperation, group work, and input from everyone involved helps to solidify our community of lifelong learners.

Figure 8.4

SELF EVALUATION

During my I-Search on _____ , I learned

how to _____ . I will be able to apply what I learned

when I _____ .

The thing I did best was_____ .

I can improve on _____ .

The people who helped me were _____ .

When I worked with them I _____ .

The thing I liked best about doing this I-Search was _____

_____

_____ .

BIBLIOGRAPHY

Armstrong, Thomas. 1994. *Multiple Intelligences in the Classroom.* Alexandria, Va: Association for Supervision and Curriculum Development.

California Media and Library Educators Association. 1994. *From Library Skills to Information Literacy.* San Jose, CA: Hi Willow Research and Publishing.

Calkins, Lucy McCormick and Shelley Harwayne. 1987. *The Writing Workshop: A World of Difference.* Portsmouth, NH: Heinemann.

Cole, Joanna. 1996. *On the Bus with Joanna Cole: A Creative Biography.* Portsmouth, NH: Heinemann.

Fogarty, Robin. 1994. *The Mindful School: How to Teach for Metacognitive Reflection.* Palatine, IL: Skylight Training and Publishing, Inc.

Guild, Pat Burke. 1997. "Where Do the Learning Theories Overlap?" *Educational Leadership* 55 (September):30–31.

Holt, Douglas. 1995. "Ring of Truth." *Dallas Morning News.*

Howe, Eleanor. 1998. "Integrating Information Technology into and Across the Curriculum: A Short Course for Secondary Students." *Knowledge Quest* 26:33.

Jackson, Norma with Paula Pillow. 1992. *The Reading Writing Workshop: Getting Started.* New York: Scholastic Professional Books.

Jansen, Barbara. 1996. "Reading For Information: The Trash-N-Treasure Method of Teaching Notetaking." *School Library Journal*, 6 (February): 29–32.

Johnson, Nancy. 1995. *Active Questioning: Questioning Still Makes the Difference.* Dayton, OH: Pieces of Learning.

Joyce, Marilyn and Julie Tallman. 1997. *Making the Writing and Research Connection with the I-Search Process.* New York: Neal-Schuman.

Kovalik, Susan with Karen Olsen. 1994. *Integrated Thematic Instruction: The Model.* Kent, Washington: Susan Kovalik and Associates.

Leech, Thomas. 1993. *How to Prepare, Stage, and Deliver Winning Presentations.* New York: AMACOM: American Management Association.

Macrorie, Ken. 1988. *The I-Search Paper.* Portsmouth, NH: Heineman.

Marrs, Carol. 1992. *The Complete Book of Speech Communication: A Workbook of Ideas and Activities for Students of Speech and Theater.* Colorado Springs, CO: Meriweather Publishing.

Nagel, Nancy G. 1996. *Learning Through Real-World Problem Solving: The Power of Integrative Teaching.* Thousand Oaks, CA: Corwin Press, Inc.

November, Alan. 1999. *The Web-Teaching Zack to Think.* Online. http://www.anovember.com/articles/zack.html.

Ogle, Donna. 1986. "KWL: A Teaching Model That Develops Active Reading of Expository Text." *The Reading Teacher* 6:564–570.

Pritchett, Price. 1999. *The Employee Handbook of New Work Habits For a Radically Changing World*. Dallas: Pritchett and Associates.

Reif, Linda. 1992. *Seeking Diversity: Language Arts With Adolescents*. Portsmouth, NH: Heineman.

Rogers, Spence and Shari Graham. 1998. *The High Performance Tool Box*. Evergreen, CO: Peak Learning Systems.

Rogers, Spence, H.J. Ludington, and Shari Graham. 1998. *Motivation and Learning*. Evergreen, CO: Peak Learning Systems.

Silver, Harvey, Richard Strong, and July Commander. 1998. *Tools for Promoting Active, In Depth Learning*. Woodbridge, NJ: Silver Strong and Associates, Inc.

Vassallo, Wanda. 1990. *Speaking With Confidence: A Guide for Public Speakers*. Crozet, VA: Betterway Publications.

APPENDIX: STUDENT I-SEARCH PAPERS

SARAH DICKERSON

Fourth Grade
March 12, 1999

MY I-SEARCH ON HORSES

Why I Chose This Topic
   I have chosen to do my I-Search on horses. There are many reasons why. The first reason is because I love horses. They are my favorite animals and are fascinating and beautiful. They are so tame and gorgeous.
   The second reason is that I love to ride them. They are so swift and easy to ride. They are also simple to train and are nice and gentle. This will be a good topic for me I can tell.

What I Knew
   Before I started my I-Search about horses, I already knew that horses are mammals and are sweet and gentle. Also I knew that horses can be trained to do many neat things. I knew that horses eat a whole lot of food such as oats, carrots, apples, hay, grass, water, salt licks, and celery. Also I knew horses can use their tails to swish flies off their backs. And last but not least, horses hate to be washed but love to be brushed.

My Search
   My search was fun but it was more challenging than anything else. The first thing I did was on March 3, 1999 I went to the library with my class and looked for books and encyclopedias on horses. I looked on the shelves and couldn't find a thing. I went back to the table where the other girls that were doing horses were sitting and I saw that they had all the books! So I borrowed their books and got a lot of information. I got all of what I needed and I filled my summary boxes up. Then we went again the next day and I found even more information.

I went to the library and got some pictures off the computer. I got about 20 pictures. Over the weekend I went to the public library and found out more information. I got some pictures off their computer. I had all of my information, and I was through with my summaries so I went to the bookstore and got two books. I went home and they were phony bologna! They weren't any good. So I took them back. I went home and looked in my encyclopedias and found more information. I then decided to interview my dad and my grandpa. They both told me the same things. I wrote them down. When I got home, I told my mom about my day. My mom said she knew a little about horses so I interviewed her and she gave me a little more information. I wrote it down and I went to bed that night feeling satisfied. That is how I did my search.

What I Learned

During my I-Search I learned a lot about horses. I learned how fast they can run, how many types there are, and whether or not they can get heart attacks, who first rode a horse and do they like to be ridden. I also learned how long before the babies can walk, how much and how many things a horse can eat and drink, and their pregnancy cycle.

Horses can run up to 42 miles per hour. The cheetah can run up to 70 miles per hour! That is 28 more miles than a horse!

Horses like to eat hay, grass, oats, corn, carrots, salt licks, turnips, apples, celery, weeds, flowers, and wild flowers. That's a lot of different things to eat.

Most horses mate in the spring. Babies are born the next spring. Racing horses usually have babies January 1 because the owner has to get them trained for the races. The owner weans the foal and puts it with other foals.

When a baby foal is born, its legs are wobbly. It tries to get up. It takes a lot of effort but eventually the foal gets up about an hour after it's born.

Horses can get heart attacks and may die from one. Most horses can get the same things we can.

There are more than 60 types of breeds of horses. Arabian horses are one of the oldest breeds. Arabian, Quarter Horses, Morgan, Lippizaners, and Thoroughbreds are the most popular breeds.

Horses love to be ridden, but are fussy when you ride them at their meal time! They start acting up and are difficult to ride at that time. The Indians first rode horses to get around and to hunt and run away from enemies.

Horses are very fascinating animals as you may have noticed from my report. As you may know, horses are one of the most beautiful animals in the world. That is what I learned about horses.

Bibliography
1. Dickerson, Arthur. Interview. March 5, 1999.
2. Fowler, Allan. *Horses, Horses, Horses*, pg. 10 © 1992.
3. Liptis, Augustis. "Raising Horses," *World Book Encyclopedia*, pg. 358 © 1998.
4. McClung, Robert M. "Breeds of Horses" *The New Book of Knowledge*, pg. 244 © 1998.
5. Podendorf, Illa. *Baby Animals*, © 1981.
6. *The Learning Company*, Inc. © 1997.
7. *World Almanac*, pg. 107 © 1997.

EMILY LAQUITARA

Fourth Grade
April 12, 1999

MY I-SEARCH ON DISNEY WORLD

Why I Chose This Topic

I chose to do my research on Disney World for many different reasons. The first reason is I have wondered what it's like to go because I have never been to Disney World. I think it would be a wonderful place that my whole family could enjoy. The second reason is I can get tickets for a cheap price because my dad's friend's dad works at Disney World in the band. But soon he's going to work at Disney Land instead.

What I Knew Before I Started My I-Search

Before I started my I-Search on Disney World I knew that there are two theme parks called Disney. There is Disney Land and Disney World. I knew Disney World is in Orlando, Florida. I also knew that there are Disney characters like Mickey Mouse that are at Disney World. You can get their autographs. I also knew that Disney World is larger than Disney Land because a World is bigger than a Land. Disney World would be a bigger place to visit.

The Search

Starting my search on Disney World was difficult but it got easier. The first thing I did was I went to the library with my class and headed for the computer to find out if they had any books on Disney World. They didn't so I went to the encyclopedia and got the D book and looked up Disney World. All that was there was stuff on Walt Disney the man. It also had stuff on the history of Disney World, but that was not one of my questions. I wasn't getting anywhere, so I got Mrs. Lockhart to see if she could help me. She did but she could not find anything either. By this time I was frustrated, so I decided to get my brochures and look. I found all kinds of information to my question. Mrs. Lockhart found a number that I could call for more answers to my questions. So that night I called and talked to a man named Talbot. When I was done I thanked him and went to eat. The next day at school I told Mrs. Lockhart I finished and all I had to do now was my summary boxes. That is what I did to find my research answers.

What I Learned

During my I-Search I learned a lot of interesting information. I learned the cheapest hotels, best souvenirs, the busiest time of the year, and how much money to bring. I also learned a good place to eat, cheapest way you get there, comfortable clothes, and also the best rides.

The cheapest hotels in the area of Disney World are the Disney's All-Star Sports, Music, and Movie Resorts. They run in the range of $74.00 to $94.00. Each room can fit 4 adults inside because of the size of the beds. They include a food court dining, heated pools, and a pizza delivery service. It is located near the Disney's Magic Kingdom, Blizzard Beach, and Disney's Wide World of Sports. The best souvenirs to get are a Mouse Musketeer hat because you can get your name sewn in it. You can also get a T-shirt with a Disney character on it. Also let's not forget an autograph book for when you meet a Disney character, you can get their autograph like you do when you meet someone famous. The busiest time of the year is summer. Summer is busy because kids get out for summer break and some kids go on vacation to the beach. At Disney World they have a beach. It is called Blizzard Beach. The amount of money to bring is about 50 dollars per person because you have to have food to eat. If you wanted to buy something like a souvenir you can. A good place to eat in Down Town Disney is the Rain Forest Café. It is about $10.00 to $20.00 to eat there. They serve sea food and American food. They do not serve breakfast but they are open at 10:30 A.M. and close at 11:00 P.M. The building is very colorful and has very detailed sculptured animals that look almost life-like. The restaurant has a store inside of it that you can buy things at. The cheapest way to get to Florida is by car. It is $200.00 per person round trip on an airplane and only about $100.00 to take a car. A car is cheaper because all you need is a car with a good gas mileage, a place to sleep on the way there, and food. If you are going 60 or 70 miles an hour you could get there in 24 hours. Comfortable clothes to wear are shorts, a T-shirt, and walking shoes if it is hot. If it is cold, wear a jacket and long pants and do not forget walking shoes. You have to wear comfortable shoes so when you walk your feet don't hurt and you won't get blisters. The most favorite rides in Disney World are Space Mountain, Splash Mountain, Dumbo the Flying Elephant, and the Tea Cups. Space Mountain and Splash Mountain are favorites because they go fast and are exciting and people like those kinds of things. The Tea Cups and Dumbo the Flying Elephant are favorites because all ages enjoy such a magical experience.

Disney World is an interesting place to visit with so much fun things to see, ride and explore. I loved to research it and I will be able to use my research when I go to Disney World this summer.

Bibliography
Disney, Explore a New Species of Theme Parks! © 1999 Pamphlet + Video.
Talbot, Phone Interview, April 2, 1999.
Disney World Travels. [Online] www.disney.com, April 5, 1999.

LORI WOJCIECHOWSKI

Fourth Grade
April 12, 1999

MY I-SEARCH ON SOCCER

Why I Chose This Topic
I chose to do my research on soccer for many reasons. The first reason is that one time I went to a Dallas Burn's game with my team. They were doing lots of passes, tricks, and shots at the goal. They were really great, everyone was cheering them on! The second reason is because I wanted to know how big the field is that they play on, how big the balls are, how much you get paid a game, and how far you have to kick the ball. Those are the reasons I have picked the topic of soccer.

What I Knew Before I Started
Before I started my I-search on soccer, I knew that you had to run a lot and pass a lot. It teaches you about team work. You wear shin guards so if someone kicks you in the shin it won't hurt as much. You have your uniform to tell your team from the other team. Your uniform includes your shirt, shorts, and your socks. You also can't wear any jewelry because if you do the ball could hit and poke a hole in your neck. I also know that you have to be at least four or five to play soccer. I also know that the balls are different sizes. Also, the field and goals are different sizes every year.

The Search

My search on soccer was fun and somewhat hard. On March 31, 1999 I went to the library to skim and scan. I found a book and an encyclopedia. It didn't really give me any information, then we had to leave. So we had put the books that we found in the middle of the table for tomorrow. The next day I worked on the computer and tried to find more books but I didn't. I felt like I wasn't getting anywhere. The next day I looked through the books and got two questions answered. I thought that I was doing pretty good now. Then the next day I didn't get anymore questions answered. I still needed more information. That night I called my coach and asked him if he could help me. He said he could. He gave answers to five of my questions. I now have seven questions answered. The next day I faxed the Dallas Burns, they faxed me back and said that they would try to get my questions answered as soon as possible. I only needed two more question answered. They faxed me back two days later.

What I Learned

During my I search I learned a lot of interesting information on soccer. I learned how big the ball is, how much you run, how big the field is, what training you go through, how big the goal is, how much you get paid, and what's the best girls team to be on.

The ball is 27 to 28 inches round. The balls weigh little less than a pound. It is a size five. The teams that are in my league are: Rockets, Fire, Alley Cats, Angels, Jazz, Fire Crackers, Lady bugs, Little Foxes, Orange Crush, Dixie Chicks, Extreme, Starburst, Red Hots, Peppers, Blue Jets and Indianetts. In professional soccer the University of Wisconsin women's team is the best girls team. Professional soccer players get paid $24,000 to $250,000 a year. The professional soccer players have to run 4–7 miles a game. The field is 116 yards by 71 yards. You have to run 90 minutes a day for training. You have to do that for a week. You have to know all the soccer skills. You also have to do all that for 8 hours a day. The goal is 24 feet wide and 8 feet tall.

You have to be able to pass to a teammate. You also have to be able to receive a ball and shoot. Professional soccer players have to travel a lot. Soccer is a very fun sport. I learned a lot from this report. There are a lot of things that you have to do to be a professional soccer player.

Bibliography

J Couch interview © 1999, April 7, 1999.
Dallas Burns Interview, fax © 1999. April 13, 1999
Federation Soccer States United © 1985, page 2–3.

CYNTHIA GAYTON

Fifth Grade
February 24, 1995

WHY DO KIDS TAKE DRUGS?

What I Knew (and Didn't Know) Before I Started My I-Search

Before I started my I-Search I knew kids took drugs because some of their friends took them. I really didn't know why kids wanted to take drugs and ruin their lives.

Why I Am Writing This Paper

I am writing this paper because I have always wanted to know why kids would take drugs and die. I was interested in this because I would always hear about how it hurt people who had a family member that died because of drugs.

The Hunt

First I started my hunt, by sharing my question with the class. That helped me get started. They told me places I could go or who to interview. Then I went to the school library on Monday and got a dictionary. That didn't help me at all. J. R. was looking through books and found a book on Marcia's and my topic. That book helped me a lot. The book was called, *Health and Drugs*. I thanked J. R. a lot of times for giving me that book. Then on Tuesday I went on looking for a different book. Marcia found one. It was called *Drug Abuse*. Marcia said she would let me use the book. I thanked her. That book helped me get more note cards done. Then I interviewed some kids on Thursday. I asked Chris F., Marcia M., and Kristen T. three questions. I thanked all of them for helping me. Then I went on and interviewed a grown-up on Friday. I interviewed her over the phone. I really wanted to interview a cop, but I couldn't. All the cops were really busy. So instead of interviewing a cop, I interviewed someone else. My sister. She used to have a friend on drugs. She was a kid. These interviews helped me a lot. I think I have my answer.

What I Learned

I learned that kids take drugs because they think it will solve all their problems and make them cool. Also kids are curious about drugs and want to see what they are like. I also learned that it is easy for drug pushers to cheat kids on giving them more money. Drug pushers always say the first drug is free. Then they have to pay if they want more. After the drug pushers get kids to start taking drugs the kids start stealing money from their parents to get more drugs. After the kids are hooked on drugs it is very hard to try to get them to stop. Some kids even die from drugs. After kids die they leave their family really hurt. Sometimes the kids' parents are the one to blame. The parents don't give their kids too much attention. Now I know why kids take drugs. I still don't know why they would ruin their lives on drugs. Maybe, I will find out when I get older.

Bibliography
Baldwin, Dorothy. *Health and Drugs*. Florida: Rourke Enterprises, 1987
Fradin, Dennis. *Drug Abuse*. Chicago: Children's Press, 1988.
Gomesz, America. Personal Interview. Houston: Feb. 14, 1995
Martinez, Marcia. Personal Interview. Houston: February 16, 1995.
Trevino, Kristen. Personal Interview. Houston: February 16, 1995.
Ford, Chris. Personal Interview. Houston: February 16, 1995.

WENDI YOUNGBLOOD

Fifth Grade
February 25, 1995

WHAT ARE THE GENERAL THINGS THAT BELUGAS DO TO EAT, SLEEP, MATE AND LIVE IN THE ARCTIC COLD?

What I Knew (And Didn't Know) Before I Started My I-Search

I knew about my question and a little about the Beluga. I knew more vivid information on my topic. I knew about the general eating habits and living life in the coldest Arctic waters. I didn't know about their migrating and sleeping habits.

Why I Am Writing This Paper

I'm writing this paper because I went to San Antonio to Sea World two years ago. They had a show about Beluga Whales and I thought they were unusual and neat. The melon was round and strange. A man was standing on it and the Beluga was picking him up and down. I thought it was interesting. When we started our I-Search I thought of all the neat things I saw. I thought of the Beluga.

The Search

My search was long and hard, but I finally got information. I went with my class to the library for the first day and looked for the topic, Belugas. I had no help on that so I looked for White Whales that didn't help either. So my hopes were lost as I looked for the last time. I looked in whales and found three books with Belugas and checked them out. It was like finding buried gold and having a ship after you. I had no time to write them up so I took them home. I found one book that just had pictures and the other had a few sentences like two each. I wrote them down in my pathfinder and looked in my Grolier's Encyclopedia and found pictures, but only two sentences. I waited until the next day for my class to go to the library and found five encyclopedias and one more book. We got to stay in the library for a longer point of time and I got to copy some information on my note cards and the page numbers down before we went to class. I had hopes that would be all I needed for my I-Search, but the information only lasted seven note cards. I found a book of all the animals in the world from Mrs. Lockhart and she let me borrow it. I got the note cards from that. I finally finished my search by writing down the information I had already known that took two cards. I slowly revised my work and added the final note card to my stack.

What I Learned

I learned many different things about the Belugas. A baby Beluga has a small melon when they are born, but it is not young enough to produce sounds. The adults migrate to the fresh waters to mate. They stay with the one mate for up to three years. The Beluga can be sixteen to twenty-four feet long and weigh up to twenty-four hundred pounds. The adult is all white and the calves are reddish brown with gray spots. They eat schooling fish, squid, crabs and lobsters, but they mostly eat bottom food. They live in the Arctic waters and migrate to mate in the warmer waters in the Spring. The average age is thirty-five to fifty years old. The snow white whale has a robust body with a small head. Their prominent "melon" forehead overhangs a small beak. Unlike most whales, their neck vertebra is not fused, which allows them to move the head freely from side to side and up and down. This is believed to help them surface and navigate through the ice flows. They are warm blooded mammals and are well adapted to the Arctic environment. They are kept warm by the thick layer of insulating blubber and have no dorsal fin, possibly to prevent heat loss. The Beluga resembles humans when giving birth. A female gives birth to a baby Beluga with other pregnant females helping with the birth. Male Belugas are immediately ready for mating once they leave their mothers. That's at twenty-eight months. They sleep at the top of the water and use their melon to float them up for air and down to rest but they never open their eyes during this process.

Bibliography
Danbury, Kevin. "Whales of the Sea," *New Book of Knowledge*. 1984 ed.

Dietz, Tim. *Whales and Man*. New Hampshire: Rorack and Dunn, 1987.

Harrison, Sir Richard. *Handbook of Marine Mammals*, West Minister, Ca. Academy Press, 1989

Leatherwood, Stephen. *Whales and Dolphins*. San Francisco: Harper and Row, 1989.

Patent, Dorothy. *Whales Giants of the Deep*. New York: Holiday House, 1984.

Dosell, Elsa. *Whales and Other Sea Mammals* Chicago. Children's Press. 1963

Ridgeway, Sam H. *Handbook of Marine Mammals*. London: Academy Press, 1989.

Reeves, Randall R. *Whales and Dolphins*. San Francisco: Harper and Row, 1989.

Watson, Lyall. *Whales of the World*. New York: Bantam Doubleday Dell, 1981.

Whitfield, Dr. Philip. "Belugas," *New Book of Knowledge*. 1984.

My I-Search on Rain Forest Trees

Written and Illustrated by Courtney Wagner

Third Grade

Dedicated to my teacher Mrs. Lockhart and my family

1. Why I Chose This Topic

I chose Rain Forest trees because we were about to learn about them. So it gave me an idea.

2. What I Knew Before I Started

Before I started my I-Search I knew that there were lots and lots of animals and trees in the rain forest. I knew some trees in the rain forest were about 200 feet high, but I wanted to know if they could get taller. I knew there were a lot of trees. I want to find out how tall can they get and how big is the beautiful rain forest. I also wanted to know how old they are.

3. The Search

The first day Mrs. Lockhart took us to the school library I found two books but only one book gave me a little information. That weekend my mom and I went to the Temple Public Library and I found four books. Out of all the books I only got three books that gave me good information. It was fun looking for information.

4. What I Learned

I learned a lot about rain forests. Trees in the rain forest are old. One tree even lived to be 4,600 years old. If you lived 4,600 years you would be really old.

Most rain forests have lots of trees. In some forests there are more than 200 different kinds of trees. If one family had fifty different people you would get them all mixed up. So you would probably get the trees mixed up. All those different kinds of

5.

trees are tall, too. They are between 200 to 364 feet. That's tall! Also all the tropical rain forests are near the equator. If a rain forest was near the arctic the trees would be dead.

6. My Project

To show what I learned about rain forests I made a big book. I began my project by going to K-mart. We bought markers, tag board, stick glue, and a stapler. Then we went to the teacher store and bought some big and small rings. That night I did the first page. I did the big book with light pencil. Then I went over it with a sharpie and colored it in. I worked on it every day. My mom helped a little but not very much. It took a lot of time but I got it done. It was fun!

7. Self Evaluation	8. Bibliography

During my I-Search I learned how to research. I will be able to use what I learned again when I do another research project.
 	
    I feel like I did a good job on my project. I included all the things I found out about rain forest trees.
 	
    The thing I did best was the big book. Next time I could do a better job on the search. The thing I like the most about doing this project was drawing the pictures in the big book.
	Jennings, Jerry. *Tropical Forest,* 1992
	
	Ketchum, Richard M. *The Secret Life of the Forest.* 1970
	
	Academic American Encyclopedia. 1985

My I-Search
on
Deer
Written and Illustrated by
Justin McLearen
Third Grade

Dedicated to my dad because he helped me a lot

1. Why I Chose This Topic

I chose deer because my dad has shot two does. I have never shot one. I don't even have a rifle. I think deer are cool animals. When me and my dad went turkey hunting there were three does standing in the road. When we got around the corner we saw three more does eating in a field. It felt so cool when I saw the deer. It was like I was standing next to them.

2. What I Knew Before I Started

I've been hunting with my dad. I watch Buckmaster every weekend. I knew that the meat of deer is called venison. White tails cover the most land in North America. Some does even grow antlers. The deer cousin are Antelope and Giraffes.

3. The Search Is On

On the first day I looked through my dad's deer book but I only found a couple of things. I felt scared. That same day Mrs. Lockhart took us to the school library. I found ten books. I was so glad. It was like winning the lotto. The next day I found two answers to two of my questions. I was so glad. April 18th I looked through four of the books and found tons of information. I was so happy. On April 20th I interviewed my dad. I answered all my questions. I was so excited.

4. What I Learned

I learned many things about all types of deer during my I-Search. I was able to answer all of my questions.

I learned that the American Moose is gigantic. Also, deer can live almost anywhere except Antarctica.

Imagine having seven kids at a time. A Chinese Water deer can.

I learned that a moose is no lightweight. Some Bull Moose can weigh up to 1,800 pounds. Deer are not cuddly animals. One guy got lucky when a deer attacked him and

5.

only got bruised.

Also, deer aren't slow pokes. Deer can run 20 to 40 mph. Now that is fast. I loved researching about deer. I will be able to use what I learned when I research again.

6. Project and Presentation

I made a poster to show what I learned about deer. I made the poster by cutting out pictures from my dad's old magazines.

On April 25th 1997 I presented my project. I was scared at first. I hoped I would not be first but Mallory was. I was sixth. I was so glad when I was finished. I think I did a good job.

7. Self Evaluation	8. Bibliography
During my I-Search I learned how to use the card catalog. I will be able to use what I learned when I research again. I feel like I did a good job on my project. I included all the things I found out about deer. The thing I did best was my poster because it was super organized. Next time I could do my researching better. The thing I liked most about doing this project was researching because it was a big challenge,	Clancy, Hary. *White Tailed Deer*. 1991. Dingwall, Laima. *Nature's Children*. 1986 McLearen, Jay. Interview, April 12, 1997. Poclan, Tom, "Deer", *The World Book*, 1994 Discovery Channel, "When Animals Attack", 1992.

# My I-Search on Chocolate ## Written and Illustrated by Emily Cleveland Third Grade	## Dedicated to Chocolate Lovers of the World
### 1. Why I Chose this Topic I am interested in chocolate because I like Chocolate and want to know what's in it. I also want to know how to make it and to find out how many different kinds of chocolate there are.	### 2. What I Knew Before I Started Before I started my I-Search I knew that chocolate is made from cocoa beans. I also knew that there are lots of different kinds of chocolate and that chocolate melts quickly in the sun.
### 3. The Search On my search I went to the school library. I looked in the card catalogue. I found some books, but they were all fiction. One was not, so I looked for it. But I couldn't find it. One of my class mates brought me a book but it didn't help me. So I thought I was getting no where. But I didn't give up. Then the next day, Pablo saw some stuff about food and called. I looked through it, but there was nothing. I spied some encyclopedias and found some information.	### 4. We had to go so I got the encyclopedia. I wrote down the information, but it wasn't enough. So my dad got some stuff on chocolate on the Internet. We also went to the Temple Public Library. I got five books. Three of them didn't give me any information. The other two gave me wonderful information. I looked in our encyclopedia. It gave me some information. I was finally ready to start.
### 5. What I Learned First of all chocolate is made from cocoa beans that grow in pods all over the trunk and branches of a cocoa tree. It may sound different, but that is the way pods grow. Chocolate contains cocoa beans, fat, protein, iron, and several, vitamins, and minerals. It also contains salt and spices. I learned that chocolate isn't bad for you. It tastes good because it has sugar in it. Lastly, I learned that there are over 2,000 different kinds of chocolate.	### 6. My Project To show what I learned about chocolate I made a big book. I began my project by getting some construction paper. I got a lot in case I messed up. Then I got my grandma to help me. She started to write down the words for the book as I told her what to write. After that we got some candy bars and ate them. We put the empty wrappers on the cover. Finally, we drew the pictures and colored them. We put the yarn in place and were finally done.

7. Self Evaluation	8. Bibliography
During my I-Search I learned how to research. I will be able to use what I learned again when I do another project. I feel like I did an amazing job. I included all the things I found out about chocolate. The thing I did the best was the researching. Next time I could do the writing even better. The thing I liked best was learning about CHOCOLATE.	Ammon Richard. *The Kids Book of Chocolate*, 1987. P. 6-13; 66-69 Bagget, Nancy. *The International Chocolate Cookbook*, 1991, p 1&2. Boyton, Sandra. *Chocolate the Consuming Passion*, 1982, p.13-19 Hearn, Machael Patrick. *The Chocolate Book*, 1983, p.33 Internet, Chocolate Lovers Home Page Internet, Hershey's Home Page, *History of Chocolate*. Internet, Godiva Chocolate, *A Glossary of Chocolate and Baking Terminology*. *Encyclopedia Britannic*, 1982, p.878 The World Encyclopedia, 1994, p. 518&519

INDEX

Note: Page numbers in boldface indicate figures.

ABOUT THE AUTHORS

LAURA LOCKHART

Laura is a teacher, district curriculum facilitator, and staff development specialist. She presents workshops on I-Searching, brain-based learning, and the reading/writing process. She has worked in several school districts teaching third, fourth, and fifth grades and has served as an assistant principal. In the 1998–99 school year, she was elected as teacher of the year at North Riverside Elementary in Keller, Texas. She is married to Jordan and has a daughter, Mallory Margaret.

DONNA DUNCAN

Donna is the director of library services for the Mesquite Independent School District in Mesquite, Texas. Previous to becoming a director, she was a teacher and then a middle school librarian. Throughout her career she has written curriculum, coordinated staff development, and presented workshops on a variety of subjects that include Integrated Library Programs, Interdisciplinary Curriculum, and I-Searching. Presently, she is the chair-elect for the Texas Association of School Library Administrators. She is married to Bob; has two daughters, Laura and Lisa; one granddaughter, Mallory; and two dogs, Max and Barney.